Trading Spaces

$100 to $1,000 Makeovers

Editor: Brian Kramer

Senior Associate Design Director: Ken Carlson

Project Editor and Writer: Jan Soults Walker

Contributing Editor: Amy Tincher-Durik

Contributing Art Directors: Chris Conyers, Chad Johnston, Beth Runcie, Joe Wysong, Conyers Design, Inc.

Contributing Writers: Amber D. Barz, Kellie Kramer

Contributing Project Designers: Susan Andrews; Carrie Hansen; Rebecca Jerdee; Cathy Kramer, Cathy Kramer Designs; Patty Mohr Kramer; Jilann Severson; Donna Talley, Ivy Vine Design

Contributing Photographers: Bob Greenspan, William Hopkins, Scott Little, Michael Partenio, William Stites, Rick Taylor, Paul Whicheloe (Anyway Productions Inc.)

Illustrator: Michael Burns

Copy Chief: Terri Fredrickson

Copy and Production Editor: Victoria Forlini

Editorial Operations Manager: Karen Schirm

Managers, Book Production: Pam Kvitne, Marjorie J. Schenkelberg, Rick von Holdt, Mark Weaver

Contributing Copy Editor: Jane Woychick

Contributing Proofreaders: Sue Fetters, Heidi Johnson, Brenda Scott Royce

Indexer: Beverly A. Nightenhelser

Editorial and Design Assistants: Kaye Chabot, Karen McFadden, Mary Lee Gavin

Meredith₀ Books

Editor in Chief: Linda Raglan Cunningham

Design Director: Matt Strelecki

Executive Editor, Home Decorating and Design: Denise L. Caringer

Publisher: James D. Blume

Executive Director, Marketing: Jeffrey Myers

Executive Director, New Business Development: Todd M. Davis

Executive Director, Sales: Ken Zagor

Director, Operations: George A. Susral

Director, Production: Douglas M. Johnston

Business Director: Jim Leonard

Vice President and General Manager: Douglas J. Guendel

Meredith Publishing Group

President, Publishing Group: Stephen M. Lacy

Vice President-Publishing Director: Bob Mate

Meredith Corporation

Chairman and Chief Executive Officer: William T. Kerr

In Memoriam: E. T. Meredith III (1933–2003)

TLC (The Learning Channel), TLC (The Learning Channel) logo, *Trading Spaces*, and the *Trading Spaces* logo are trademarks of Discovery Communications, Inc., used under license.

The decorating projects and how-to instructions set forth in this book are not necessarily endorsed or recommended by the *Trading Spaces* designers and are intended instead to illustrate some of the basic techniques that can be used in home decorating.

***Trading Spaces* Book Development Team**

Kathy Davidov, Executive Producer, TLC

Roger Marmet, General Manager, TLC

Tom Farrell, Executive Producer, Banyan Productions

Sharon M. Bennett, Senior Vice President, Strategic Partnerships & Licensing

Carol LeBlanc, Vice President, Marketing, Strategic Partnerships

Erica Jacobs Green, Publishing Manager

Elizabeth Bakacs, Creative Director, Strategic Partnerships

Trading Spaces

$100 to $1,000 Makeovers

Meredith® Books
Des Moines, Iowa

contents

$ **cha ching**

more bang **decor**

3 p.m. on Day 2
of a *Trading Spaces*
Makeover, Anyplace, USA:

The *Trading Spaces* crew—including Paige, the designers, and various production team members—huddle around piles of paper, shuffling through receipts and the occasional napkin with jottings. A production assistant meticulously itemizes expenses within a spreadsheet on a laptop. The final price tags for two room makeovers mount ever higher at the bottom corner of the computer screen. This is serious business.

S o yes, television fans and decorating skeptics alike, *Trading Spaces* really does pay attention to final budgets. "Sure," you may be saying to yourself, "but do they really get all that done for $1,000?" The answer? Well, yes and no.

Most tools and supplies, such as paintbrushes and roller trays, are not calculated into the budget; the show assumes most households would have these on hand. And because the show is geared toward do-it-yourselfers, the cost of skilled labor and professional interior design assistance isn't figured into the total. However, the stuff of the makeover—all the bold paint, fabulous fabric, great flea market finds, and strategic furniture purchases—must cost $1,000 or less.

Trading Spaces makeovers are proof-positive that a small sum of money can produce amazing results. Choosing the perfect paint color, cozying up a sofa with an exceptional set of pillows, adding a band of satin ribbon to a window treatment—each of these decorating options is simple and inexpensive, yet the potential impact is tremendous.

Trading Spaces $100 to $1,000 Makeovers gives you all the tools, tips, and tricks you need to create amazing before-and-after transformations of your own—without breaking your bank:

▶ **PART I: DOLLARS AND SENSE** gives you the skinny on how to create a budget, find inexpensive (yet totally cool) furniture and accessories, and stretch your decorating dollar.

▶ **PART II: MAKEOVERS BY THE NUMBERS** offers a guided tour of 14 fabulous rooms featured on *Trading Spaces* and *Trading Spaces: Family*. In these examples you'll see

you can save some extra money.

Packed with insider hints and savvy shopping tips and topped with a hefty dollop of *Trading Spaces* sass, this is your step-by-step guide to creating showstopping spaces at bargain-basement prices. With *Trading Spaces $100 to $1,000 Makeovers* at your side, you're ready to dream about, plan, shop for, and execute a complete transformation without spending a penny more than you plan. (Who wants to be grilled by Paige about going over budget during Designer Chat?!)

Get inspired. Get budget-smart. And get going on your way to a totally new, completely you space!

for your . . . . ating buck

how the *Trading Spaces* designers make $1,000 look like $10,000.

Room Redo shows four rooms made over on three budgets: $100, $500, and $1,000.

Thrifty Project Inspired by the Show describes the materials and skills you need and the steps you need to follow to create high-impact decorating projects all by yourself.

From the Designers sidebars give your favorite decorating daredevils an opportunity to weigh in on money topics.

▶ **PART III: BUDGET WORKSHOP** helps you get your financial house in order before you ever lift a paintbrush. Easy-to-use worksheets help you estimate how much projects will cost and discover places where

money management the trading spaces way

Investors on Wall Street may think they're tops in giving out financial advice, but decorators know that the *Trading Spaces* crew has the corner on putting limited decorating dollars to work.

▶ **NO COST.** Each *Trading Spaces* room redo comes with a message: Very little money—and sometimes no money at all—is required for a dramatic makeover. Check out the wonderful furniture arrangement Vern came up with for an Asian-inspired, texture-rich living room (page 54). Sure, the furnishings look expensive, but the placement of the pieces is what makes the room functional; this approach could be duplicated without the cost of new furniture.

▶ **LOW COST.** Sometimes the biggest bang comes with the smallest price tag. For example, in Vern's study makeover, black and white photocopies of lighthouse photographs provide graphic punch (see page 39).

▶ **FOCUSED COST.** The *Trading Spaces* designers also know how to invest their decorating dollars in exactly the right places to produce the most impact. Make note of the brick-look flooring Hildi installed in a chic Florida living room (page 134). Brick, stone, tile, or hardwood flooring is a major investment; however, in the right place, a great-looking floor can yield big design results for years to come.

Hamlet said, "The play's the thing." Turn the page for a little fun comparing your makeover to a Broadway production. First get familiar with the characters and discover your budgeting habits. Next learn how to set the stage. Then see if you can identify the players in action and discover ways to finish projects affordably in phases. Study the checklists for tips on where to find advice and help—for free or at low, low prices—and where to hunt for bargains. Finish up by browsing through a gallery of flea market fix-ups; let them be the muse for your next decorating play.

sense

the play's the thing

Fortunately, funding a room makeover isn't nearly as costly as bankrolling a Broadway production. Producing a play and producing a dramatic room makeover are projects that do have some similarities, however. Find out if you fit somewhere in the cast of characters, *opposite*, then read on to learn how you can set the stage for dramatic style and rave reviews—all within your budget. Get ready, because the curtain is going up!

It's near the end of a typical *Trading Spaces* episode, and Paige is visiting with one of the designers: "I have bad news," she says, frowning. "You've gone over budget." Sometimes the designer's eyes open wide in surprise; more often, the designer sighs and admits, "I know." Whether a designer loses track of the budget or runs out of time to return a few items, the result is the same. In seasons 1 to 3 of *Trading Spaces*, the overspending had to be paid out of the designer's pocket to the host. In season 4 of *Trading Spaces* and in *Trading Spaces: Family*, however, the designer must remove items from the room to ensure the redesign is within the spending limit.

Although you may not hear much about the budget until the end of a *Trading Spaces* episode, in the real world you need to determine your budget up front and keep a close eye on how much you're spending throughout the process. (The *Trading Spaces*

designers do this too; the cameras focus more on the action and entertainment of the makeovers and less on the planning.)

To figure out how much money you'll need for supplies and materials, turn to the "Budget Workshop" that begins on page 142. This collection of tips, worksheets, and calculators will help you peg down costs before you shop, so you'll know how much cash you realistically need to get the job done.

Also check out the cast of characters, *opposite*, and see if you recognize anyone. Though the personality descriptions are tongue-in-cheek, you'll find some nuggets of truth in them. Use what you discover about your money attitudes to help keep spending in check or to encourage yourself to spend a little more freely, depending on your budgeting character.

Then, with your own budget and spending style in mind, turn the pages to learn how to decorate in layers and phases.

have you seen these people?

You may recognize yourself in one or two of these characters. Make an honest assessment and use what you learn to improve your budget decisions.

POLLY B. PRUDENT

is very careful with money—maybe even a little too careful. Polly has been saving, saving, saving for a long time and wants to be certain she has all the cash needed to finish the project.

▶ **POLLY'S REVIEWS:** Polly earns four stars for her financial foresight, but she gets lower ratings for delaying her dreams so long. If you see yourself in Polly, remember that leaving a few things undone is OK. Get started transforming the room now and finish the details later as money becomes available. That way, you'll be enjoying your new space sooner than you thought. Besides, as you page through this book, you'll discover some low-cost ways to complete your dream makeover.

SAM A. SPENDTHRIFT

has holes in his pockets. Every time Sam visits a store, he totes home something for a room redo. Soon the garage is overrun with stuff. Where will it all go?

▶ **SAM'S REVIEWS:** Sam earns only one star for budgeting; however, he gets five stars for keeping an eye out for decorative features. Still, Sam needs to balance budgeting and buying. If you see some of yourself in Sam, note these guidelines:

▶ If you spot an item you love and it's one-of-a-kind (such as a vintage chair), check whether it fits your budget; if it does, buy it—even if you're not sure where it might work into the scheme. The reasoning is, you may never find another like it. The trick is to not overdo these kinds of purchases.

▶ If you see a more ordinary item that's appealing, and you're not sure it will work in the room, delay the purchase. You can always buy it later. However, if the item is at a rock-bottom price, it might be wise to quickly determine whether the piece can help you achieve your decorating goals. If it can, grab the bargain.

▶ Make a shopping list of items you absolutely need to complete the room; then stick to your list. Use this book to help you buy only what you really need, at the best price. Resist the urge to splurge and you'll end up with a clutter-free room that reflects good planning.

PAM PROCRASTINATOR

can't seem to make decisions about a room makeover. She also hasn't figured out how to pay for what she needs.

▶ **PAM'S REVIEWS:** Poor Pam—her lack of performance means no review. If you find yourself putting off redecorating because you're not sure where to begin and how to budget, you're in the right place. This book is jam-packed with affordable, doable ideas that will motivate you.

BART BIGBUCKS

has plenty of cash to create his dream room. He tackles the project with gusto. What will the results be?

▶ **BART'S REVIEWS:** Bart earns four stars for enthusiasm. His story could end well or badly:

▶ **Tragedy:** Bart spends far more than necessary and ends up with a space that looks ostentatious and overdone. Even Bart isn't comfortable in his made-over space.

▶ **Happily-ever-after:** Bart realizes that strategic spending works better than overspending. His room reflects a balance of splurges and bargains—and it is the perfect place in which to spend time with friends.

If you have a nest egg waiting in the wings, congratulations! Figure out a short list of most-desirable splurges—for example, an armoire and a fireplace—and make those special purchases. Continue to use the advice and ideas in this book to keep your budget in check. That way, you'll have cash left for a great vacation after all the work is done!

BACKGROUND

PRIMARY PURCHASE

ACCENTS

Any great play features three components: a terrific set, charismatic stars, and talented supporting players. When you set out to do a room makeover, think of your room as a stage and consider the key elements that will appear there: The background is your stage set, the primary purchase is your star, and the accents are supporting actors. You'll learn how to balance and layer these elements so your makeover stays on budget and achieves marvelous style.

A Broadway producer has to decide where to invest the budget. Will the bulk of the bucks go toward the star's paycheck? Or will this play be known for its breathtaking sets? Perhaps an important supporting role will require a well-paid actor.

As an investor in your own little home production, you get to decide where to funnel the finances—or how to slice the decorating pie, *above*, so to speak. The decorating pie can be sliced in a variety of ways, depending on your goals and interests. To allocate your budget, consider the pieces of the pie and decide how big you'd like each piece to be:

▶BACKGROUND. Think of your room as an empty stage waiting for the set director (that's you!) to make the transformation. What role do you want the four walls, the ceiling, and the floor to play? Do you want them to serve as the driving force of the room with brilliant painted hues, powerful pattern, or glimmering metallic leaf? Or do you want the background to be quiet and understated?

Your answer will depend on your ultimate goals for the room. Consider the players that will come onstage next—your primary purchase, such as a large sofa or a bed, and the accessories and accents you want to add to the scheme. If you know you want a drop-dead gorgeous sofa to be the highlight of the room, for example, downplay the background and invest a good chunk of your cash in your primary purchase. The walls can still sport great color; find a bold color chip and then take it down a notch or two to let the sofa stand in the spotlight. If you're reusing an existing sofa and you're not thrilled with its look, choose a sophisticated solid-color slipcover and invest in a dramatic pattern or color on the walls, ceiling, and floor.

For example, in Mississippi: Winsmere Way, *below left,* Hildi dressed the walls of a bedroom in dramatic red toile fabric—with results that are well worth the significant expense. A bed, sofa, and decorative items in the room take on lesser roles. The sofa— a thrift store find—helped Hildi stay on budget. A curving armoire that was custom-built to keep costs down adds grandeur to the room without upstaging the walls.

To see another example of a successful background investment, turn to page 38. Vern transforms an ordinary office into a handsome library retreat by dressing the walls in moldings and various shades of green and brown.

▶ **PRIMARY PURCHASE.** Sometimes your primary purchase will logically serve as the focus of the room; the bed in a master bedroom is one good example. (The bed in a guest bedroom, however, doesn't have to be the focal point. Instead a writing desk or small sitting area may get the spotlight.) If the bed will be the most important object in your bedroom makeover, then treat it as such, as Frank did in San Diego: Duenda Road, *below center.* There, moldings and long swaths of fabric surround the bed, giving it due prominence.

Invest in a spectacular footboard and headboard if you wish. Or put your dollars toward high-quality linens, an ultrathick comforter, and armloads of plush pillows. Employ accents to draw more attention to the bed. Hang an impressive piece of artwork above the headboard, for example, or invest in an amazing canopy with yards of luxurious fabric draped all around the bed. On page 30 Kia employs a seashell-inspired bed to create a fabulous focal point for the room. On page 70 Hildi makes an 11-foot-long sofa—swathed in yards of pink python-print vinyl—the star of her room.

▶ **ACCENTS.** It's easy to think of accents and accessories as the jewelry you might use to dress up a simple black dress. Arrange a few decorative boxes, a vase, and some books on a console table, and you've added enough detail to take the look beyond ordinary. If you're a collector, however, the small things may be the most important items in your room. In an office in Vegas: Smokemont Court, *below right,* Edward put the focus on a musician's instruments by placing them in prominent locations—even hanging a guitar on the wall and shining a spotlight on it.

You may decide to keep your backgrounds subtle and spend your dollars on a primary purchase designed to showcase your collections. For example, purchase plenty of shelves or a handsome display cabinet with well-planned lighting to show off your treasures. You'll find two great examples of accents in action in this book: Doors and doorknobs become the theme of a great-room designed by Christi on page 62. Turn to page 86 to see how Edward builds a bedroom around an Oriental icon.

▶ **BACKGROUND:**
MISSISSIPPI: Winsmere Way

▶ **PRIMARY PURCHASE:**
SAN DIEGO: Duenda Road

▶ **ACCENTS:**
VEGAS: Smokemont Courts

players in action

Now see if you're able to spot whether the background, the primary purchase, or the accents are the main focus.

▶ **DESIGNER:** Doug
▶ **THE SITUATION:** A young boy's small bedroom
▶ **FOCUS:** Who could miss the *primary purchase* that dominates this space? Two halves of real cars make this bedroom a little boy's dream come true. One car holds a bed in its trunk, and the second car is waiting to be equipped to serve as a toy box. (Doug ran out of time to finish this part of the project.) The background and accents play an important secondary role in the room; for example, a toy car zooms along a painted highway on one wall.

▶ **DESIGNER:** Hildi
▶ **THE SITUATION:** A plain white family room
▶ **FOCUS:** The *background* takes the lead role in this design scheme. Hildi uses dozens of vinyl records with colorful labels to establish a fun and funky theme. A trip to the thrift store yielded this one-of-a-kind look for a mere $60.

▶ **DESIGNER:** Gen
▶ **THE SITUATION:** A family room in a new house with a cookie-cutter fireplace
▶ **FOCUS:** A French poster proved a stylish beginning for this *accent*-focused family room: Gen repeats black from the diva's dress throughout the room and carries the golden yellow poster background to the walls. Other special artwork and accents draw the eye around the room.

▶ **DESIGNER:** Christi
▶ **THE SITUATION:** A family room with no special focal point
▶ **FOCUS:** A *background* of torn scraps of brown paper glued to the walls launches a rustic Old West-inspired setting. The black-painted gunslingers silhouette becomes the playfully exciting focal point.

▶ **DESIGNER:** Vern
▶ **THE SITUATION:** A family room with a white stucco fireplace that doesn't suit the house
▶ **FOCUS:** Slate tiles are the starring *primary purchase* in this family room; Vern rehabs a homely fireplace with a new slate facade to create a striking focal point. The fireplace is now a favorite gathering spot, so the slate was a good investment.

▶ **DESIGNER:** Edward
▶ **THE SITUATION:** A small but promising space occupied by college-age guys
▶ **FOCUS:** Snowboards earn a prominent place on the wall alongside a funky green lava lamp. A vibrant purple backdrop pairs up with a deep red band of color along the baseboard to make these hip *accents* pop.

▶ **ALSO REMEMBER:** The focus of a room can be changed easily. Bring out the background, for example, with the addition of a dramatically different coat of paint.

to the finish— in phases

Divide your room makeover into phases, and you can complete the room more affordably by paying as you go. The job is less intimidating too if you break it into these manageable bites. Follow along as *Trading Spaces* shows you how with ideas from past episodes!

start

phase 1

▶ **BACKGROUND:**
MISSISSIPPI: Winsmere Way
Painting walls and the ceiling is one of the least expensive ways to make a big change. For a few dollars more, moldings and decorative three-dimensional pieces give walls even more personality; Doug's work illustrates the point, *left*. Before buying paint, choose the fabric for the room (a swatch will do if you don't yet have the budget to buy the fabric); then use it as inspiration for choosing paint colors. It's much easier to match paint to fabric than vice versa.

phase 2

▶ **BUILDABLES:**
ARLINGTON, VA: First Road
Begin constructing stylish pieces that make your room more functional. An armoire is ideal for concealing the television and stereo equipment or for storing clothing, books, and other items. Alternatively, customize the interior to serve as a dry bar or a sewing center. Doug made the exterior of this armoire chic, *left*, with fabric applied in pleated folds. If an armoire is too rich for your budget, start with smaller projects, such as side tables, a coffee table, and storage cubes. Remember that MDF is your budget friend.

phase 4

▶ **LIGHTING:**

PENNSYLVANIA: Sterling Drive

Review past episodes of *Trading Spaces* and study the lighting in this book (see pages 124–125 for two more bright ideas); then devise your own lighting projects. Affordable lamp kits and other lighting supplies are available at home centers and lighting stores. Purchase plain shades for bargain prices at discount stores and use crafts store finds to customize the shade. Remember that candles, as shown *left*, make any room more beautiful for only a few dollars.

phase 5

▶ **MAIN ACCENTS:**

VEGAS: Woodmore Court

Your room is really coming together now. Have fun finding accents that you love. Flea markets, garage sales, thrift stores, and discount stores all offer a huge selection of low-cost accessories. Select items that will personalize your rooms and employ *Trading Spaces* ideas for big impact. For example, place multiple images in symmetrical arrangements, as Gen did *above*. Save money by finding frames on sale and using calendar images or even photocopies as the artwork.

phase 3

▶ **SEWING:**

PENNSYLVANIA: Sterling Drive

Now you can pull out the fabrics you collected and begin sewing window treatments, slipcovers, pillows, and duvets. If you are a novice, pillows are an ideal easy project for honing sewing skills. Even if you don't own a sewing machine, you can tackle many fabric projects with iron-on hem tape. Look for hem tape at crafts and fabric stores and follow package directions.

phase 6

▶ **FINISHING DETAILS:**

PENNSYLVANIA: Sterling Drive

Scan your room for areas that could use small flourishes, such as a finial, *left*. Your investments in this phase can be minimal and spread out over time. Use painted details (such as stencils), ribbons, fringe, cording, and other adornments to spice up walls, furniture, cabinets, and window treatments.

finish

free (or low-cost) help ▲

The more advice you obtain for your room makeover, the more time and money you'll save. Check off the resource ideas that you like best and then go out and seek assistance.

▶ HOME CENTERS

☐ **Employees.** Home center employees are some of the most knowledgeable folks around. Ask them where the bargains are, when the next sale is scheduled, and how to do particular tasks yourself to save money.

☐ **Friendly customers.** Contractors and hard-core remodelers are wandering the aisles with you. Strike up a conversation and you may glean valuable advice and money-saving tips.

☐ **Workshops.** Most home centers offer free or low-cost workshops on a number of projects. Learning new skills such as laying tile, installing lighting, hanging wallpaper, or painting a faux finish may take only a few hours of your day.

☐ **Samples/literature.** Home centers offer free printed information and samples for you to take home and try out.

☐ **Interactive displays.** Larger home centers now offer high-tech displays that let you play with computer-generated room designs and palettes. Have fun mixing and matching finishes, fabrics, window treatments, and much more—all on your own for free.

▶ DESIGNER SHOWROOMS

☐ **Ideas on display.** Decorators sometimes use room displays to showcase their abilities and style. These displays are often excellent free resources for gathering ideas.

☐ **Helpful employees.** Chat with the designer on duty and share aspects of your project. You may receive a few tips to make your plans better.

☐ **Free or low-cost literature.** Check racks near the door or the sales counter for free or low-cost information on decorating elements you need for your room makeover.

▶ OTHER MEDIA

☐ **Television.** The tube is rife with home decorating and how-to shows, including *Trading Spaces*, of course! Tune in and take notes.

☐ **Radio.** Some talk shows dish out tips and advice for would-be decorators.

☐ **Newspapers, special sections.** Watch for inserts promoting local home shows and other events. These sections are good sources of low-cost advice. Some papers feature a weekly "Home & Garden" section.

▶ SPECIALTY RETAILERS

☐ **Flooring.** When you buy your flooring, find out if the store offers free installation instructions or instructional videos.

☐ **Lighting.** If you spend a certain amount, some lighting stores will provide a lighting plan for free.

☐ **Lumber.** Need ideas on how to stretch your buildables budget? Ask the people at the lumberyard for ideas on managing your costs, such as substituting MDF for plywood.

☐ **Kitchen and bath.** Showrooms that specialize in cabinetry or plumbing fixtures and fittings will sometimes provide free computer-generated floor plans for efficient layout. Home centers may provide a similar service.

☐ **Crafts.** Explain your ideas to the employees of a crafts store, and they can guide you to the necessary supplies, help you find the best deals, and offer advice. Crafts stores also offer workshops that focus on particular crafting techniques or materials.

☐ **Appliances.** Knowledgeable appliance salespeople can provide you with all kinds of advice on which models to buy and how to install them yourself.

☐ **Paint.** Buy the best paint you can afford. Talk to employees to find out what makes their paint the best or to learn which brands are popular and why.

☐ **Furniture.** Furniture salespeople can offer advice on how to choose durable furniture and fabrics. Some stores have designers who can help you plan a room arrangement for little or no cost.

LIBRARIES AND BOOKSTORES

- [ ] **How-to books.** Look for reliable publishers and check out books on projects.

- [ ] **Magazine articles.** Find titles you trust and skim articles for ideas. Check out or purchase publications that offer specific projects or techniques you plan to incorporate.

- [ ] **Lectures.** Watch newspapers for announcements about visiting authors. Attend their lectures to gather information and advice on how-to and decorating topics.

- [ ] **Internet access.** Libraries usually provide free Internet access—often on high-speed lines. If you don't have a home computer or have a slower dial-up connection, a visit to the library can kick your online research or purchasing into high gear.

- [ ] **Videos/software.** Libraries often have extensive how-to video and software collections.

▶ HELPERS

- [ ] **Teens and college students.** Young people need jobs; you need help. Strike a bargain and gain a helper.

- [ ] **Trade with neighbors.** Help your neighbors paint; maybe they'll help you install tile.

- [ ] **Have a party.** Invite a group of friends to a painting party. Feed them well.

- [ ] **Barter with a pro.** For example, if you don't own the tools to build shelves but have sewing skills, make a deal with a carpenter who needs slipcovers.

▶ CONTINUING EDUCATION

- [ ] **Classes.** Through community colleges and adult continuing education programs, learn how to upholster, make slipcovers, lay tile, use power tools, and master other how-to skills—all for very little money.

- [ ] **Teachers.** Chat with the instructors after class to glean additional insider's tips and ideas.

- [ ] **Other students.** You may find some students who are knowledgeable about your topic of interest. Have a cup of coffee with a few good prospects and discover some fresh ideas.

- [ ] **Helpful texts.** The books that instructors choose to augment their courses may be affordable and worthwhile additions to your do-it-yourself library.

▶ FABRIC STORES

- [ ] **Mix and match.** Need help combining various fabrics, colors, and prints? For many fabric store employees, mixing and matching fabrics is second nature.

- [ ] **Fabric selection.** Ask the store employees to help you determine the best fabrics for your window treatments or the sturdiest buys for upholstery projects.

- [ ] **Bargains or sales.** Employees can point out good buys in the bargain bins and tell you when the next sale will be.

- [ ] **Novelties.** Fabric stores often have the latest in trims, ribbons, and buttons. Speak to store employees to find out what's new.

- [ ] **Can't sew?** The fabric store is still the place to go. Ask employees how to adapt your ideas into no-sew projects.

▶ INTERNET

- [ ] **Do-it-yourself websites, personal home pages, and message boards.** The Internet overflows with information on decorating projects and techniques. Read from a variety of sources and be on the alert for misinformation.

- [ ] **Associations.** Go to association websites, such as for sheet goods manufacturers, to access an abundance of quality how-to information.

- [ ] **Manufacturers.** Their websites often feature tips on selecting and using products. Many manufacturer websites now include calculators to figure how much of a material you need; they may also feature interactive mini-programs that let you paint a room, try out new flooring, and do other virtual makeovers.

- [ ] **Retailers.** Retailers sometimes offer online articles that serve up great decorating ideas. Seasonal and online-only sales are available around-the-clock.

- [ ] **Magazine- and book-related web pages.** Your favorite magazines and book publishers often have complementary websites to augment the advice and projects offered in their printed publications.

shop smart

Bargains aplenty are out there if you know where to look. When hunting down supplies, materials, and other elements for your makeover, consider the following resources and tips.

▲ Always keep your eyes open for a great buy. You never know when you'll encounter a sidewalk, garage, or warehouse sale.

▸ **WHERE:** Thrift Stores (Goodwill, Salvation Army, and a variety of local outlets provide a wealth of used items at great prices.)

▸ **WHY:** These stores offer some of the most fun and rewarding shopping experiences around.

▸ **TIPS:** Visit often to check for newly stocked items, such as upholstered pieces that are ready to slipcover and coffee tables, end tables, and dining chairs that are ready to paint.

▸ **WHERE:** Flea Markets

▸ **WHY:** Flea markets are often vast and crowded; however, the bargains lurking there make the hunt worthwhile.

▸ **TIPS:** Visit flea markets to find unusual accessories, furnishings, and vintage linens and fabric remnants.

▸ Learn how to negotiate prices with vendors. Ask politely, "Is this your best price?" or "Could you do better on this price for me?" With this approach you'll likely receive a lower price.

▸ Learn to let go. If you can't get a great deal on a particular item, let it go. In most cases something equally good—if not better—will

turn up at another booth or flea market.

▸ Bring supplies with you. If possible bring along strong canvas or plastic shopping bags to carry all your purchases.

▸ Plan your transportation. Travel to flea markets in a vehicle large enough to carry your purchases home. If you don't own a van or truck (and don't want to rent one), ask a dealer who won't budge on price if you can get free delivery or shipping.

▸ Bargain with a buddy. Sometimes dealers will give you a better deal on an item if you and your friend purchase multiple items from their booths, especially if the two of you pay with one check or credit card.

▸ **WHERE:** Damaged Freight Area

▸ **WHY:** Some home centers, furniture stores, and appliance outlets (as well as other types of specialty stores) offer damaged freight at reduced prices.

▸ **TIPS:** Call around. Save gas money and time by using the phone to find out which stores in your area sell damaged freight.

▸ Patience is a virtue. Be willing to sort through a stack of sinks, layers of countertops, boxes of ceramic tiles, or dozens of doors, for example, and you may find what you want with only minor damage that's nearly invisible—for 50 to 75 percent off the retail price.

- Bargain. Offer a lower price and see what happens. Most stores are eager to clear out damaged goods.
- Buyer beware. Keep in mind that damaged goods are often sold "as is," meaning no warranty, no returns, and definitely no refunds.
- Sleuth out other damaged goods. Damaged goods aren't always labeled or placed in a designated area. Sometimes you'll find less-than-perfect items on the shelves with the good stuff. Point out the damage to the salesperson and find out if the store will offer a discount.

▶ WHERE: Building Supplies Recyclers and Salvage Yards

▶ WHY: Some communities accept, store, and sell used lumber, sheet goods, hardwood flooring, windows, doors, cabinetry, and other materials and supplies.

▶ TIPS: Check local listings. Turn to the phone directory first and call around to find salvage yards in your area. If you can't find a listing in the phone book, waste collection companies may be able to tell you who is recycling building supplies in your area.

- Bring wheels. If you'll be moving anything heavy, bring along a dolly, a wheelbarrow, or a wheeled cart to ease the chore.
- Bring bigger wheels. Drive a vehicle that can transport what you buy. If you don't own a pickup, borrow or rent one for the job.
- Think differently. An architectural element that you discover can be used for something other than its original purpose.

Old doors and windows, for example, make interesting decorative accents.

▶ WHAT: Floor Models

▶ WHY: If you don't mind that several thousand people have opened and closed that dishwasher or refrigerator door over several weeks or months, you may be able to purchase the appliance from the home center for much less than retail. The same goes for furniture floor models at department and furniture stores.

▶ TIPS: Ask if floor model appliances, plumbing fixtures and fittings, cabinetry, countertops, and furniture are for sale.

- Find the clearance center. Many national chains designate one retail location per region as the destination for all unsold clearance items and floor models from the stores in the area. Ask a manager at your favorite retailer if a regional clearance store exists in your area.

▶ WHAT: Discontinued Lines

▶ WHY: Manufacturers and retailers want to unload discontinued items to make way for new seasonal lines.

▶ TIPS: Ask employees if discontinued models are available. They'll often take you to a back room or special section designated for discounted merchandise.

- Keep watching. Discount stores introduce, promote, reduce the price of, and discontinue new product lines quite quickly, sometimes within a matter of weeks. Shop your favorite stores frequently and pay attention to product lines you like. When the line goes on sale or clearance, buy up the remaining items at a significant discount.

track down tools

Many of your shopping trips will include forays to find the right tool. You need certain tools all the time—a hammer and a drill, for example. Other tools are rarely used and yet crucial to particular projects. Stretch your budget with these ideas:

▶ **BORROW.** After all, what are neighbors for? Why buy a reciprocating saw when you plan to remove only one stud wall in your lifetime?

▶ **TRADE.** If you never use your router, find a friend or family member willing to trade you a tool you really need, such as a drill.

▶ **RENT.** Some tools are costly to buy, yet you need them to achieve professional results or to get the work done in a reasonable amount of time. If you know you'll use a tool very infrequently, such as a floor sander, rent it instead of buying.

▶ **LEARN A NEW SKILL.** If you enjoy handiwork and you want a workshop that's equipped to the nines, consider teaching yourself a new skill. Hire out your newly acquired talents and tools on weekends to earn dollars for your own room makeovers. Buy a high-quality diamond-tipped saw, for example; then cut marble and other rock-hard materials and tiles and install floors and countertops for some extra cash. You can also hire out skills/tools that you already have and then use the dollars to buy the new tools that you need.

favorite flea market fix-ups

Use this collection of insider's secrets inspired by the show to create high style without spending a bundle. Use items you already have on hand or treasures from flea markets or garage sales.

▶SALVAGE

▶MAP IT OUT

▶FRAMED FIX-UP

▶**SALVAGE.** Visit architectural salvage yards to find special features that will dress up your room, such as moldings, fireplace surrounds, columns, windows, doors, brackets, cabinets, hardware, sinks, and stair railings. Call demolition companies to find out if they are scheduled to tear down any old houses. They may let you into the house to rescue features for bargain prices. Also, keep an eye out for neighbors who are remodeling. They may have architectural pieces that they are willing to give away. Watch the curbs on garbage day—some people throw away usable materials.

▶**MAP IT OUT.** Maps, both old and new, provide inexpensive decorating material. Photocopy maps from an early geography book and tack the copies to the walls for an interesting background. (You may be able to use wallpaper paste to secure maps to walls. Test a spot first to see if the paste smears the image.) Hang an antique school map as a window shade (or have a copy store photocopy a map onto canvas). Wrap each end of the map (or canvas photocopy) around a wooden dowel. Set the top wooden dowel inside roller-shade brackets mounted inside the window frame.

▶**FRAMED FIX-UP.** Less-than-perfect cabinets take on new character when you repaint and reface the doors with framed art, such as botanical prints, family photos, or pages torn from an old calendar. Drill pilot holes through the frames and into

▶TEATIME

▶LADDER DISPLAY

10 Must-Haves for the bathroom

Throughout this book, the "10 Must-Haves" list the most-needed, most-wanted features in various rooms. Use these lists to help you choose the elements you want. Following are the top 10 features an ideal bath would offer:

1. **The perfect color scheme.** A flattering and soothing or cheerful color scheme helps you start the day out right.

2. **Counter space.** Dual vanities are all the rage, so work them in if at all possible. If your bath won't accommodate two vanities, consider adding a second vanity in the bedroom.

3. **Storage.** Maximize the storage you have with organizational tools, such as wire bins and divider trays. If possible add open shelves and more cupboards. Update cabinet exteriors with new paint or stain and new hardware and moldings.

4. **Mirrors.** The bath is the only room designed for primping, and mirrors enhance the opportunity. Purchase large mirrors that fit your budget and style; they'll make this small room feel larger.

5. **Task lighting.** Good task lighting helps keep you out of the shadows. You'll look better and you'll see better for everyday routines such as shaving or brushing your teeth.

6. **Sunlight.** Natural light is the best light for primping. Take advantage of the sunlight the room already enjoys by using strategically placed window treatments and mirrors.

7. **Privacy.** Choose window treatments that will protect your right to privacy.

8. **Extra outlets.** Hair dryers, electric razors, curling irons, and rollers all need to be plugged in, and occasionally, you want them all plugged in at once.

9. **Fluffy towels and enough bars or hooks to hang them on.** Being able to use as many big, fluffy towels as you want is a luxury you owe yourself. If you install enough towel bars or hooks, your housemates and guests might actually consider using them.

10. **Candles.** These wax wonders are great to have on hand when you want to indulge in a luxurious soak.

the doors; then secure the frames to the doors with drywall screws. If you grow weary of the image in the frame, undo the screws and substitute a new photo or print.

▶**TEATIME.** Flea markets, garage sales, and even Grandma's attic are great places to find beautiful vintage tea towels, napkins, and aprons for only a few dollars each. Showcase your finds by stitching them into decorative pillows.

▶**LADDER DISPLAY.** Use a pair of painted wooden brackets to hang a vintage ladder horizontally on the wall. Drape the ladder legs with antique quilts or vintage linens or install hooks for hanging teacups or other collectibles.

▶HIDE-A-FILE

▶SET THE HOOK

▶HIDE-A-FILE

▶BATHROOM BEAUTIFIERS

▶**HIDE-A-FILE.** Filing cabinets are a necessary evil, and usually these metal monsters aren't pretty. Place same-size cabinets side by side and conceal them with a slipcover. (Watch for affordable fabric remnants or vintage tablecloths at flea markets, garage sales, and auctions.) Position the covered cabinets beside your desk to serve as an additional surface for office-related items as well as for books and treasures on display. If you don't sew, join the seams of the slipcover with iron-on fusible hem tape. Or avoid the task of making hems entirely by using tablecloths instead. Drape the tops of the cabinets with a suitably sized tablecloth; then add a second tablecloth (folded in half lengthwise) as a skirt. Use adhesive-backed hook-and-loop tape to secure the skirt around the tops of the filing cabinets.

▶**SET THE HOOK.** Old mismatched flatware can be found by the boxful at garage sales and auctions or maybe in your own storage. Bend the handles of old forks or spoons and secure them to the wall with finishing nails. To complete the look bend flatware into handle shapes and use the pieces as unconventional pulls on cabinet doors and drawers.

▶**BATHROOM BEAUTIFIERS.** Keep even a small bathroom clutter-free with this idea: Stack old suitcases and baskets and use them to hide towels and supplies. (Or use one suitcase and set it on legs or a table base.) The attractive arrangement on the wall is a bargain collection of chipped crockery lids that echo the curve and color of the sink.

▶**SHUTTER SHAPE-UP.** Window shutters in all shapes, sizes, and colors dot salvage yards and flea markets. Hang a short one on the wall for organizing bills and other mail or purchase a wider one for holding magazines and catalogs.

▶**PANEL DISCUSSION.** These pressed-tin ceiling panels cost only $40 at a flea market. Attached to a wood frame that holds them away from the wall, the panels serve as a handsome headboard.

▶**CORRAL COSMETICS.** Install a mirror in an old picture frame—this frame looks especially charming still dressed in the original paint. Lay the frame on your dressing table to round up cosmetics and other vanity supplies.

▶**BOTTLES OF BEAUTY.** Gather a collection of old bottles and enjoy the shapes and color variations. This collection rests on an old lap table used for writing.

Sometimes you absolutely must splurge on something special to make your room perfect. When you spend a good chunk of the budget on one thing, however, you have to perform a balancing act with the bucks. The *Trading Spaces* designers have learned to walk the fine line between splurges and bargains, as these examples illustrate.

▲SPLURGE: Doug adds a distinctive yet pricey chair to his living room design in Austin: Wampton Way. The newsprint upholstery becomes a charming focal point in the room.

▼BARGAIN: Doug extends the newsprint theme with an inexpensive custom wall art project. Colorful newspaper pages are decoupaged onto pre-stretched canvases.

▲SPLURGE: Hildi creates stunning visual impact by stapling more than 6,000 silk flowers to the walls of a bathroom in Mississippi: Golden Pond. The total cost for flowers exceeds $600.

▼BARGAIN: Hildi stays within her spending limit by using an inexpensive white terry cloth bath towel to upholster a new vanity bench. It's a thrifty choice that's perfect for a bathroom!

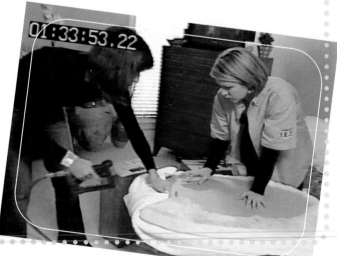

▼BARGAIN: To establish the illusion of grandeur, Gen uses an inexpensive yet effective painting trick. She brings the ceiling color down onto the walls a few inches, creating faux crown molding.

▲SPLURGE: In a Missouri: Sunburst Drive bedroom, Gen selects luxurious leather and velvet to weave a cover for an impressively sized headboard in a weave pattern.

▼SPLURGE: Vern updates a living room in Orlando: Winter Song Drive with a thrift store sectional, a surprisingly pricey purchase at $600.

▲BARGAIN: Vern manages the rest of his $1,000 budget by applying paint to a variety of surfaces, especially the remaining pieces of storage furniture.

▲SPLURGE: In Chicago: Spaulding Avenue, Hildi spends nearly 70 percent of her budget on the wood used to make a beautiful bed and bench.

▼BARGAIN: Hildi stays on budget by using pastels and hair spray to create a grass-theme wall treatment.

▲SPLURGE: After choosing cedar to build a large headboard and wall shelving unit, Gen doesn't have much money left for other items in Orlando: Gotha Furlong.

▲BARGAIN: Gen cleverly improvises by updating a ceiling fan with an inexpensive application of silver rub.

overs
numbers.

When you approach a makeover the *Trading Spaces* way, you'll never sacrifice beauty for the budget. Tour the following rooms to learn the secrets behind some of your favorite transformations; see how the designers make $1,000 seem like so much more. Check out "Wise Buys" for helpful tips on getting the best value in decorative supplies and accessories. "Money Crunch" sidebars provide dozens of alternative, low-budget decorating ideas. You'll also find four room redos inspired by the show that illustrate what $100, $500, and $1,000 can do in a bedroom, dining room, kitchen, and living room.

seaworthy
sleeping

DESIGNED BY KIA

The owners of this master bedroom live near the ocean, so Kia brings the beach into their boudoir with pale ocean greens and a dramatic headboard and footboard modeled after seashells.

Pearly finish
Glaze mixed with opalescent color gives the headboard and footboard a glossy luster that recalls the inside of a seashell.

Sunset sleeper
Golden and orange hues make the bed linens seem as rich as the sun setting on the ocean. To freshen the existing comforter and save money, the gold fabric is made into a duvet cover that slips onto the comforter like a pillowcase.

Fan club

In the Florida climate, a ceiling fan in the bedroom is a bonus. Nickel-finish accents and white blades help this model blend with the tropical look of the room.

Calm seas

Choosing pale green for walls sets a serene mood. The space offers a casual, relaxing atmosphere, almost as good as a private beach.

Tropical accent

Traditional moldings wouldn't do in this room. Instead, bamboo poles, split in half, stand in as tropical accents on the wall flanking the bed.

Pillow puff

To stretch the budget, flat existing pillows gain a little fluff from batting that is wrapped around each pillow and held in place by the pillowcase.

Stepped-up shelves

A pair of bamboo poles leaning against the wall support small shelves and add another inexpensive touch of the Tropics.

Happy as a clam

A headboard and footboard shaped like seashells make the ocean connection clear. Fabricating the pair from MDF keeps them affordable.

►before

▶**Miami: Ten Court**

Deep blue carpeting, dark-stained wood furniture, and even darker blinds and draperies add up to a space that is, well, dark. An animal-print bedspread and peach walls date the room, and the bright red toolbox—though innovative as a television stand—belongs in the garage, not the master bedroom. The homeowners ask Kia to let in the light.

From the Designers

▶**KIA STEAVE DICKERSON**

Q What is one aspect of a room worth splurging on?

A In my kitchen, I splurged on flooring. My kitchen is 30 feet long and 20 feet wide, and I put down australian cherry floating laminate. The flooring ended up costing about $5,000, but it just makes the room look amazing. To balance the flooring expenses, I painted walls and cabinets, changed door hardware, and attached new laminate on top of existing laminate countertop.

Q If you only had $100 to pump up the style of a room, how would you spend your money?

A I'd buy two gallons of high-quality paint and one gallon of tinted primer. I'd spend the rest on four rolls of wallpaper border. I think wallpaper border is the most cost-effective way to get a dramatic transformation along with paint.

Q What can you do if you love international style but don't have much of a travel budget?

A You don't even have to leave your own home. Go on the Internet and do some research. Find out what is significant in China and what says India and what says Japan. And then start to hunt and find those things that speak to you about that country.

Married more than 16 years, the owners of this master bedroom said they were ready for a romantic retreat—though the husband didn't want to part with his red toolbox television stand! Fortunately, Kia kicked the toolbox out of the scheme and brought the ocean and beach indoors, starting with soft ocean green on the walls. Moldings and shelves fashioned from bamboo emphasize the tropical seaside theme and the bed introduces oversize seashell shapes. Breezy sheers at the windows let the sunshine in—one of the top requests of the homeowners.

◄If privacy isn't a concern and sunshine is on your wish list, window treatments fashioned from sheers may suit your style—and your budget. Here, raffia tiebacks provide a textural contrast to silky sheers, appropriately patterned with palm trees.

►Hildi helped out Kia with this thrift store find. A little paint and some new fabric for the cushion take the chair from bargain to beautiful. When you track down low-cost furniture and plan to paint it, prime first. This will ensure good adhesion and no bleed-throughs.

mattresses

Shopping for a quality mattress can be mind-boggling. To keep your task manageable, look for the two or three features that matter most to you; then base the remainder of your decision on budget and comfort preferences. If you share a bed with someone else, shop together—you may decide to buy a mattress that offers a different degree of firmness on each half. Orthopedists usually recommend choosing the firmest mattress you find comfortable.

When shopping, wear comfortable clothing and easy-to-remove shoes—and leave your dignity behind. Lie on the bed, move around, and bounce a little the way you would at home. The right mattress will support your body at every point. Five mattress types are available:

▸ **TRADITIONAL COILS.** Also referred to as an innerspring mattress, the traditional coil mattress is made of tempered spring coils covered with layers of padding and upholstery. If your budget allows, buy a mattress and box spring as a set (box springs typically cost less than half the price of the mattress). The two parts are engineered to work together; using an old box spring will reduce the comfort and longevity of the mattress.

The number of the coils determines how much support a mattress offers. A full-size mattress needs at least 300 coils; a queen-size mattress, no less than 375; and a king-size mattress, a minimum of 450. A quality innerspring mattress costs around $600 for a full-size, $800 for a queen-size, and $1,000 for a king-size. Options such as pillow-top cushioning and ticking materials affect the price and the feel, making mattress testing important.

▸ **FOAM.** Made of a solid latex foam core, these beds offer firm support without traditional coils or springs. They provide a comfortable resting spot whether set on a wooden platform or a traditional box spring. Because the foam core conforms to your body, you toss and turn less in your sleep. Prices for quality foam mattresses range from $1,000 to $3,500 depending on the size of the mattress and the density of the foam.

▸ **INFLATABLE.** These affordably priced mattresses are great when space for overnight guests is limited. Quality models plug in and inflate in minutes. Firmness is adjustable, and most inflatables stow away in a standard-size duffle bag. Prices range from $80 to $200.

▸ **WATER BED.** These old water-core standbys are available in a variety of styles, including waveless, soft-sided, and pillow-top models. Hard-sided water bed mattresses are available for as little as $100, while fancier soft-sided models range from $600 to $1,200 depending on the size and options selected.

▸ **ADJUSTABLE.** These power-operated coil mattresses are frequently advertised on television. The head and foot of the bed adjust at the touch of a button. Queen-size and larger beds feature separate controls for each side. Optional features include vibrating massage, radiant heat, and pillow-top cushioning. These beds range from $2,000 to $7,000 depending on the coil and spring quality, the mattress size, and the options you choose.

make over your bedroom

▶before

Though you're probably asleep most of the time that you're in the bedroom, your eyes deserve to open to a room that looks great. This bedroom has some decent pieces of furniture; however, the ordinary color scheme and lackluster character need a wake-up call. A botanical look with a dash of modern attitude (a design inspired by the show) instantly refreshes the room. As the available decorating dollars increase, so does the welcoming vibe and rejuvenating spirit of the room.

▶$100 budget breakdown

paint for walls (2 gallons)	$51
canvas stretchers & canvas	$40
paint for canvas	$8
TOTAL	**$99**

$100

▶**GOODBYE BEIGE.** Banish boring beige walls with a refreshing coat of spring green.

▶**CANVAS CLASSIC.** Make this beautiful headboard for less than $50. Stretch and staple canvas over a 2×2-inch frame (this one measures 62 inches wide and 56 inches tall). Paint the canvas with a base coat of creamy color; let dry. Then paint an easy design in green, such as these three large leafy branches. (If you don't like to paint freehand, trace a design onto the canvas first.) Tape off a 1-inch border all the way around and paint the desired shade. For added comfort, layer batting inside the frame before you hang the frame behind the bed.

$500

DRESSER DRESS-UP (1). Brighten the room further by giving the existing dresser a makeover with ivory paint and new sparkling glass knobs. An antique oval mirror added above the dresser plays up the vintage look. A myrtle topiary in a green pot continues the botanical theme.

CLEAR COLLECTION (2). Give the dresser top a touch of glass with a cluster of decanters gleaned from flea markets and thrift stores. Embellish the container tops with twine and fill with water and real branches.

BARGAIN WINDOWS. Search for fabric sales and soften the windows with yards of apple green fabric. (The fabric featured here cost only $10.) Hang the panels from clear shower curtain rings embellished with faux berries; thread the rings onto an iron curtain rod.

PRIVACY, PLEASE. Make easy Roman shades using cream-color burlap fabric gathered with lengths of ribbon for additional privacy.

GLOWING REVIEWS (3). Bring in subtle, low-cost lighting, such as the pair of imitation alabaster lamps on the nightstands. For mood lighting create a votive candleholder by gluing together nine glass holders, tying the grouping with braided jute ribbon, and adorning the square with a faux botanical sprig.

▶ $500 budget breakdown

dresser paint	$9
dresser knobs	$24
glass bottles (6)	$12
roll of twine	$1
green throw pillows	$42
botanical leaf comforter	$70
curtain panel fabric	$10
shower curtain rings	$6
iron curtain rods	$40
faux green berry garland	$20
cream burlap fabric	$4
ribbon	$3
plywood strips	$3
lamp & shade (2)	$60
fabric & trim for table topper	$2
glass votive holders (9)	$5
green votive candles (9)	$3
ribbon for votive candles	$3
twig trivet for votive grouping	$3
storage basket	$14
wicker tray	$12
myrtle topiary	$30
vintage mirror	$12
beige leaf sheets	$30
TOTAL	**$418**
PREVIOUS TOTAL	**$99**
NEW TOTAL	**$517**

▶$1,000 budget breakdown

flea market daybed	$75
muslin fabric	$10
pillows for sofa back	$85
plant stand	$5
potted fern	$19
11×14-inch frames (4)	$51
mat board	$16
silk green leaves	$4
burlap	$3
glass garden domes	$44
ribbon and jute	$9
pillar candles	$5
iron brackets	$20
8×9-foot sisal rug	$108
paint for rug	$12
wicker trunk	$25
TOTAL	**$491**
PREVIOUS TOTAL	**$517**
NEW TOTAL	**$1,008**

$1,000

▶**TEXTURE UNDERFOOT.** Purchase a large sisal rug and use two colors of acrylic paint to create a charming checkerboard design. (This rug features alternating squares of natural sisal, white, and green.)

▶**BE SEATED (1).** Establish a sitting area with a flea market daybed. Wrap the mattress in a few yards of oatmeal-color muslin. Fill the back with fluffy pillows to shape an inviting spot for napping, snuggling, or reading.

▶**CHARACTER COUNTS (2).** Make the sitting area more personable with a wicker trunk coffee table and a collection of framed botanical prints on the wall above the daybed. Balance the arrangement by placing candle sconces on each side; use garden domes flipped upside down as votive holders. Cradle the domes in ribbon hangers suspended from decorative metal brackets.

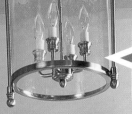

The light stuff
A new lanternlike pendent fixture plays up the lighthouse theme initiated by the framed artwork.

Trio-tone trick
Three colors make the grid composition more noticeable. Light green walls provide a subtle backdrop for brown boards topped with narrow dark green boards.

Eyes up
A pair of vases with flowers draws the eye upward, emphasizing the dramatic height of the room.

Door dynamics
An existing cabinet gains doors made of affordable MDF. Trim pieces match those on the wall for continuity.

Another dimension
Flat walls become fantastic when layered with a grid of l× boards.

Tray chic
Tray tabletops serve as bowls for displaying dimensional objects, such as these enticing red apples.

molding an image

Rustic fishing gear and a wallpaper border featuring a puppy motif compete for attention in this boxy computer room. The kids do their homework here, so the space definitely needs irresistible style; the existing cutesy themes don't cut it. The entire family is hoping for a look that's "crazy, cool, and more welcoming." Walls are the key ingredient in this redo orchestrated by Vern. Ordinary, low-cost 1× boards applied in a stylish grid give the walls depth and the room new life.

Nautical and nice
Red frames around photocopies of lighthouse photos introduce dramatic contrasting color.

before

▶North Carolina: Dogwood Trail

A dramatic high ceiling and a beautiful half-circle window are the best features of the room. The space is boxy, however, and the fishing and puppy themes don't mesh. The room lacks appeal for the kids in the family. Vern's challenge is to make this a room that the family wants to spend time in—especially because this is where the homework happens.

▲Shopping for bargains paid off in many ways in this study. Vern notes that he picked up a $60 pair of lamps (one is out of view) for $20. The shades were only $3.19. "You have to be creative with your resources," he says.

Style was barking up the wrong tree in this study. A wallpaper border with a puppy motif was the first thing that needed to go as Vern surveyed the family/homework/computer room. The color palette wasn't very doggone inspiring either. "Beige, beige, and more beige," Vern says, pulling the wallpaper border down. "We will do color."

He reveals three hues—two shades of green and a brown—that combine to warm the space and make it more welcoming. Better still, the interplay of shades highlights the new star of the space: a grid of moldings covering the walls.

Milled moldings range from low-cost to expensive depending on the detail, material type, and size of the piece; in large quantities even inexpensive millwork can add up to a bundle of money. Vern keeps costs under control in this room by using ordinary 1× boards to create the grid effect. Stacking a narrow

▶ architectural moldings

Moldings are a cost-effective way to bring architectural interest to a boxy space. Here are some ideas to build on:

▶ **IDENTIFY.** Visit the molding aisle of a home center to see the molding styles, sizes, and materials that are available. Save money by purchasing pine, which is cheaper than hardwoods, and painting the wood.

▶ **STACK.** Vern layered a narrower board on a wider one to achieve visual dimension on the walls. Build on this idea to stay on-budget. Rather than spend a fortune on extrawide crown molding, for example, create your own substantial piece by layering a variety of moldings on a 1× board. Experiment by laying various profiles on the board and shifting the pieces until you achieve the look you want.

▶ **DISTINGUISH.** To gain even more bang for your decorating buck, draw attention to moldings by applying paint or metallic leaf finishes. White paint always makes moldings stand out; for a more subtle effect, paint the wood pieces with high-gloss paint in the same shade as your matte-finish walls.

▶ **DIVERSIFY.** Move beyond baseboards and crowns. Apply moldings in a boxlike frame in the middle of the wall to create the look of raised panels. Add built-up crowns above doorways between rooms to re-create the shape of a Federal-style pediment. To get the sophisticated look of a coffered ceiling, add a grid of moldings to your flat ceiling.

◀ Vern photocopied lighthouse pictures to create this collection of classic black and white images. To make your own thrifty art, start with bargain frames. Paint them the desired color and add black and white photocopies of favorite images or photographs.

►Muted greens and soft browns create an air of serenity in the study, making it an ideal quiet space for doing homework and reading.

board on a wider board lends depth to the design, transforming the once plain study into a handsome room that has the sophisticated air of a paneled library.

The study is visible from the foyer, and originally it didn't make the best first impression. "Before," Vern says, "when you walked into the house, you would see the desk." Now an armoire catches the eye instead. Created by adding MDF doors to an existing set of shelves, the armoire is dressed in paint and moldings to match the walls. Vern also adds to an existing desk in the room by flanking it with extra desks that Carter builds from MDF.

Serving as a plush backdrop for the desks are floor-to-ceiling deep green velvet draperies. A dark green slipcover updates the existing sofa, and a pair of storage cubes topped with trays stands in as stylish coffee tables.

Black and white photocopies of lighthouse pictures—fashionably framed in rich red wood—provide standout artwork

for the room. A ceiling fixture that reminds Vern of a lighthouse provides the appropriate finish.

Vern sums up: "We were able to take a small space that really needed to be functional, but wasn't, and make it visually interesting and functional at the same time."

lightbulbs

Whether you're lighting a kitchen work surface or a romantic table for two, there is a bulb for the job:

► **INCANDESCENT.** This is the original filament-style lightbulb that has been around for decades. The color of the emitted light is warm and flattering, mimicking natural light. The light level is easily controlled by a variety of different wattages, but you should never choose incandescent bulbs that have a higher wattage rating than the fixture manufacturer recommends. Incandescent bulbs are available in decorative shapes (candle flame, downlight globe, or tubular) and in clear, soft white, and colored styles. They also come in special-use varieties including long-life and antivibration models.

► **FLUORESCENT.** Fluorescent bulbs offer a harsher, whiter light that is less flattering but more illuminating than incandescent bulbs. Fluorescent bulbs are also more expensive than incandescent bulbs but last much longer and are more energy-efficient. Fluorescent bulbs are available in long tubes and ring shapes that fit only in fixtures specified for fluorescents. They are also available as screw-in bulbs that fit many lamps and ceiling fixtures. Compact models are designed for use in special fixtures geared for tight spaces, such as undercabinet lamps, as they generate less heat and last longer than incandescent bulbs.

► **HALOGEN.** Halogen bulbs boast a bright white light that intensifies the colors in a room. Halogen prices have dropped considerably in recent years, but they are still pricey compared to incandescent bulbs. They are designed to be long lasting, but fingertip oils that contact the bulb upon installation can cut the bulb's duration in half. To help the bulb last longer, wear plastic gloves (or sandwich bags) over your hands whenever handling a new bulb. The bulbs also get much hotter than the other bulb types, so they require a greater clearance between adjacent materials to prevent scorching.

► **MOOD-ENHANCING DIMMER SWITCHES.** The ability to vary light levels can enhance the ambience of almost any room. Dimmers are available in toggle, dial, or touch-sensitive styles. Before purchasing a dimmer switch, make sure it will work with your hardwired fixture. Unless equipped with a special dimmer, most fluorescents cannot be dimmed. Some halogen lights also require special dimmer switches.

blinds, shutters, and shades

Save both time and money by selecting high-quality yet affordably priced ready-made blinds, shutters, or shades for light control. Then enhance their appearance the *Trading Spaces* way with inexpensive cornices, valances, or curtain panels—either store-bought or homemade.

▶ **ROLLER SHADES.** Affordably priced solid-vinyl roller shades or vinyl-and-fabric laminated combinations are commonplace and available at home centers and discount stores. Do-it-yourself kits for fusing decorator fabrics to solid-vinyl shades are available at fabric stores. To prevent tearing when the shade is pulled, choose a vinyl covering that is at least 6 millimeters thick. Heavier roller shades muffle light and sound better and are worth the extra cost for adults and children who sleep during the day.

▶ **PLEATED SHADES.** These shades are made of pleated fabrics in a variety of solid colors with varying degrees of translucency. They operate like blinds, without the pivoting slats.

▶ **VENETIAN BLINDS AND MINIBLINDS.** Available at home centers and discount stores, venetian blinds and miniblinds offer more options in light control than roller shades or pleated shades. Venetian blind slats measure about 2 inches wide; miniblind slats are generally 1 inch wide. Measure the depth of the window frame to determine which will fit best in an inside mount. Blinds can be raised to let in the light and view or lowered and closed for privacy. Lowered slats can also be tilted to control the light and the view. For the most privacy and light control, choose blinds that have little or no space between the slats when closed. Choose slats made from warm woods or solid-color aluminum or vinyl. Wood blinds are long lasting and provide excellent light control; however, they tend to be costly. Aluminum blinds clean easily; on the downside they are noisy to operate. Vinyl is low-cost and turns yellow in sunlight; look for sturdy hard-plastic versions, which mimic the look of wood for less money.

▶ **VERTICAL BLINDS.** Available at most home centers and discount stores, these blinds operate in the same fashion as venetian blinds and miniblinds, except vertical blinds open and close vertically instead of horizontally. Choose slats made of vinyl, fabric, or vinyl-and-fabric laminated combinations.

▶ **BAMBOO AND MATCHSTICK BLINDS.** These affordably priced blinds raise and lower like other horizontal blinds; however, the narrow bamboo reeds do not pivot. The blinds are available in both natural and painted finishes at many home centers and discount stores. Look for blinds with an additional backing layer of cloth for privacy and light control.

▶ **BIFOLD SHUTTERS.** These slatted and framed window treatments are available at most home centers. A hinge between each framed section allows the shutters to fold toward the sides of the window. Slats within each frame can be tilted to control the light and the view. Bifold shutters are typically made from stained or painted wood or solid-color vinyl.

◀ This light fixture is reminiscent of the top of a lighthouse. Home centers offer affordable light fixtures in myriad styles.

◀ Vern topped table bases with trays to make these stylish coffee tables. To make your own thrifty coffee tables, rest decorative trays on top of laminate storage cubes. (Look for interesting trays at an import store.) Add legs to the cubes, if you wish. Then paint the trays and cubes as desired.

Under $40

what you need

Materials
Dress
Matching thread
Contrasting fabric
 (about 1 yard)
Charms

Tools
Measuring tape
Scissors
Sewing machine or
 fusible webbing

dress a window

In this low-cost project you actually dress a window. Start with a shopping trip to the clearance racks at a clothing store or go to a secondhand clothing store or thrift shop; hunt down a long-skirted dress made of fabric that suits your room. Then follow these step-by-step directions to transform the dress into a fanciful window treatment. If you don't sew, substitute fusible webbing for stitches.

1. Measure the window

length and width. Purchase a dress made of medium-weight fabric and check that the length is ample for the window, allowing for hems and top folds. The circumference of the dress (measured around the hem) needs to be at least 1½ times greater than the width of the window. (A large-size dress works best for this project.)

2. Lay the dress out

on a table and cut in half vertically, making the cut down the center of the dress (see Photo A). Measure the length needed to cover the window. Add 1 inch for lower hem and ½ inch for seam at top. (For the window shown here, the back of the top section is lined to avoid folding down a 4-inch allowance at the top and losing length; see step 3. The lining adds stability to the top of the curtain.)

3. Hem the two

vertical cut edges of each half of the dress with a ½-inch allowance. Cut a piece of contrast fabric to match the width of each

A.

panel plus 2 inches (1 inch turned back at each end); make the contrast piece itself 4 inches wide. Stitch contrast piece to the top of the curtain with a ½-inch seam. Turn and press into place.

4. Cut a rod pocket strip

of contrast fabric, matching the length of the rod plus 1½ inches. Press under ½ inch on each long edge. Pin into place on curtain and stitch. Remember to tuck short edges (1 inch allowed at each end) under before you start and topstitch to finish those edges as well. This creates the rod pocket on the outside of the curtain.

5. Finish the curtain

by adding a bottom trim of contrasting fabric. This design features triangles of contrasting fabric, but you could add a straight band or scalloped edging. For additional interest sew on charms, beads, or other small decorative features. To make the triangles as shown here, cut 4-inch squares of fabric and fold them diagonally; then fold again to create smaller triangles. Stitch the triangles to the bottom edge with a single row of topstitching. Hand-stitch charms to each triangle tip.

6. Thread the rod pocket

of the curtain onto a decorative rod and hang. Sew fabric tiebacks or use metal tiebacks as shown here.

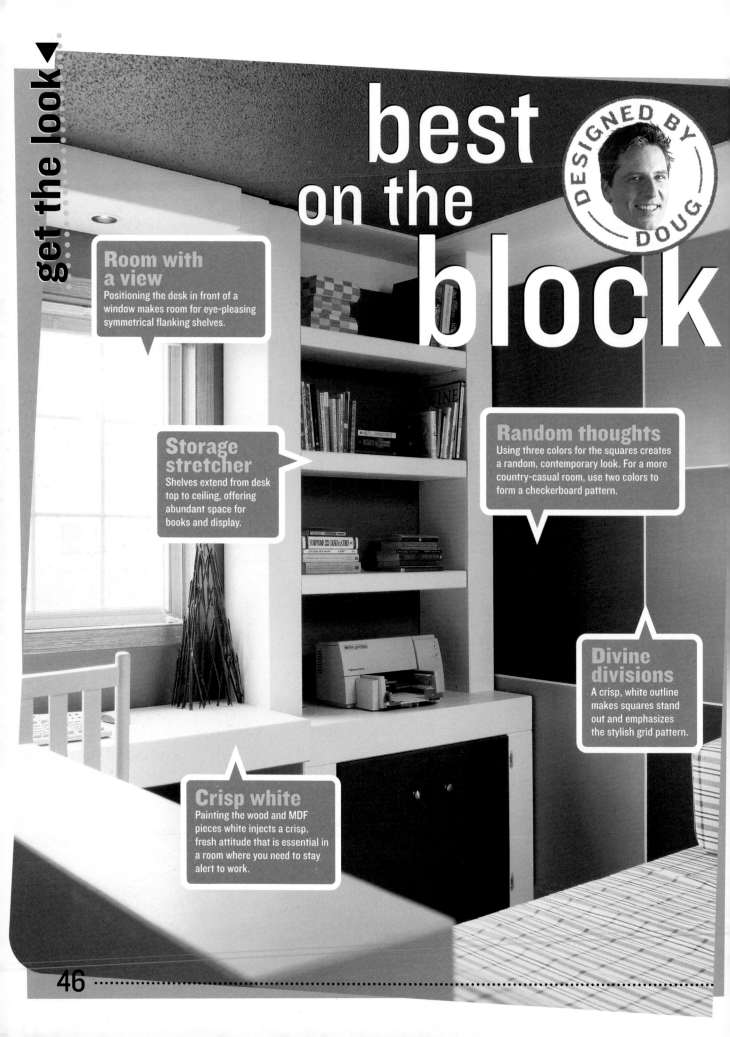

best on the block

DESIGNED BY DOUG

Room with a view
Positioning the desk in front of a window makes room for eye-pleasing symmetrical flanking shelves.

Storage stretcher
Shelves extend from desk top to ceiling, offering abundant space for books and display.

Random thoughts
Using three colors for the squares creates a random, contemporary look. For a more country-casual room, use two colors to form a checkerboard pattern.

Divine divisions
A crisp, white outline makes squares stand out and emphasizes the stylish grid pattern.

Crisp white
Painting the wood and MDF pieces white injects a crisp, fresh attitude that is essential in a room where you need to stay alert to work.

Easy trim
Even a small room benefits from architectural touches. Here two different widths of 1× board are added to the top of the wall and the ceiling to form streamlined crown molding.

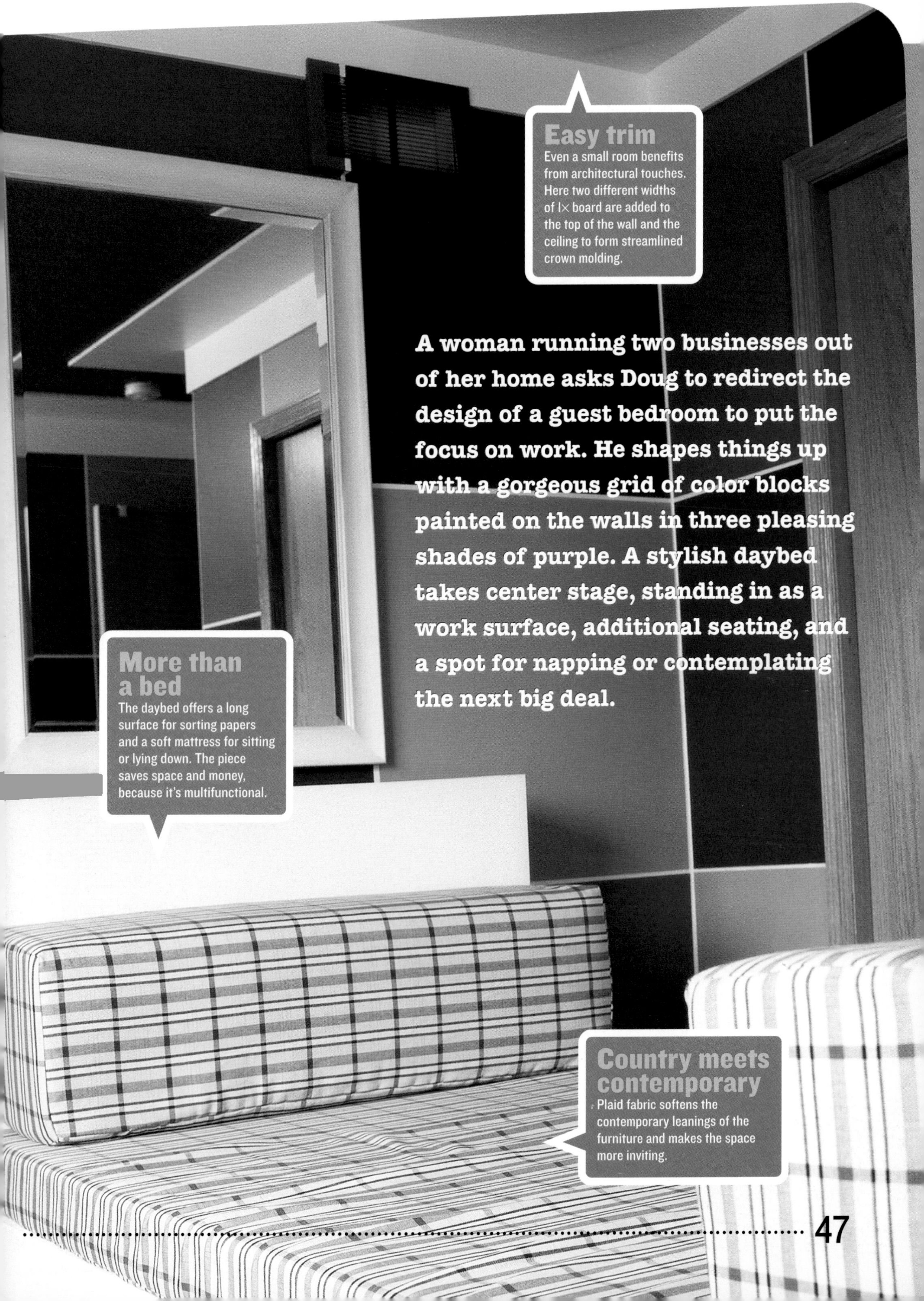

A woman running two businesses out of her home asks Doug to redirect the design of a guest bedroom to put the focus on work. He shapes things up with a gorgeous grid of color blocks painted on the walls in three pleasing shades of purple. A stylish daybed takes center stage, standing in as a work surface, additional seating, and a spot for napping or contemplating the next big deal.

More than a bed
The daybed offers a long surface for sorting papers and a soft mattress for sitting or lying down. The piece saves space and money, because it's multifunctional.

Country meets contemporary
Plaid fabric softens the contemporary leanings of the furniture and makes the space more inviting.

before

▶ **Minnesota: Pleasure Creek Circle**

**Pale green paint, a wall border, and a twin bed
make this space more bedroom than office.
The homeowner needs a place where she can
focus on her home-based businesses. She
doesn't like the current clutter and wishes for
a sleek, modern look. Doug decides to clean up
with blockbuster style.**

▲ Amy Wynn used MDF to build the
shelving unit, desk, and decorative
moldings. This readily available material
is less expensive than plywood and is
ideal for constructing cabinets,
furniture, and trim. To create the illusion
of crown molding for less money and
labor, Doug specified two widths of MDF
strips—5 inches wide on the wall and 12
inches wide on the ceiling; the pieces
overlap where the walls and ceiling meet.

Reducing clutter and getting organized are some
of the best stress reducers known to mankind.
Happily, organization and style are closely related
and can be accomplished at the same time in a well-planned
makeover. This homeowner likens her existing home office/guest
bedroom to "a walk-in junk room." She's hoping for improved
organization so she can efficiently run her two home businesses.
The space needs to be more appealing because the homeowner

will spend many hours working there. In addition, the room needs to easily convert to a welcoming bedroom for overnight guests.

Doug devises a plan to turn the window wall into a workhorse with built-in shelves, cabinets, and a desk top, all constructed of MDF. Doug orders the same material for the new daybed so it is visually compatible with the work and storage surfaces. Before any of these pieces are installed, the wallpaper comes down and a jazzy painted motif of oversize squares goes up.

Because the walls were once coated with wallpaper sizing and paste, primer is a must to ensure that subsequent coats of paint don't crackle as they dry. After the primer dries, Doug and one of the neighbors determine the size of the squares they'll paint on the walls. (They decide on 29-inch squares, which allows four whole squares to fit across the wall.) Doug and the neighbors also create a "color map" that shows where to apply the three shades of purple Doug chose for this design; the map will help them avoid painting adjacent squares the same color. A long carpenter's level and a pencil are used to easily and evenly mark off squares. Masking off the outline of the squares helps keep painted edges crisp and straight.

MDF cut into 5-inch-wide strips trims the tops of the walls, and 12-inch-wide MDF adorns the ceiling perimeter. The trim pieces give the boxy room a hefty dose of architectural interest. Painting the trim, shelves, desk, and daybed white makes them stand out against the purples and keeps the work space from being too serene.

A playful plaid-fabric bulletin board provides casual contrast to the contemporary squares; the homeowner can use the board to display photographs, greeting cards, schedules, and office-related papers. The same plaid appears as upholstery for the daybed mattress, which Doug found on sale for only $65. Though the bed didn't fit along the wall he had in mind, it works well in the middle of the room, where it functions as a spot for sorting papers, sitting, or taking a quick nap.

money crunch $

▶ tape and paint wall treatments

Create stripes, diamonds, squares, or other geometric shapes with low-tack painter's tape and paint. Here's how:

▶ **WIPE DOWN THE WALLS** to remove dust and grime. If you've recently removed wallpaper or the wall is already painted a deep color, start with a coat of primer; let dry.

▶ **PAINT ON THE BASE COAT** of color. Let dry thoroughly—at least overnight. (If, for example, you want white lines between painted squares as shown here, start with a white base coat and space squares accordingly to reveal the line.)

▶ **MARK THE SIZE AND SHAPE** of your designs, using a pencil, a measuring tape, and a long carpenter's level. If you're painting stripes or diamonds, a chalk line may come in handy. Also, if you want a design element to be evenly spaced, do the math beforehand. For example, determine how many stripes of a particular width can fit across each wall.

▶ **OUTLINE STRIPES, SQUARES, OR OTHER SHAPES** with low-tack painter's tape. Burnish the edges of the tape with your thumbnail so that the paint doesn't bleed underneath. Paint the designs the desired color. Remove the tape before the paint dries to avoid pulling up paint. Let dry.

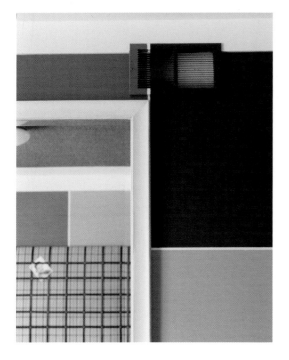

◀ In this home office the painted color blocks continue directly over built-in obstacles, such as this air-return cover, tying them into the scheme and making them less noticeable.

▶ A bulletin board like this one can hold more than messages and grocery lists. Put one in the bedroom, family room, or kitchen to display photos (of your favorite *Trading Spaces* designers, of course!), greeting cards, and other items that can be slipped beneath the ribbon strips. Cut a piece of ⅛- or ¼-inch hardboard to the desired size and wrap with batting. Hot-glue or staple the batting to the back of the board. Top with fabric and hot-glue or staple the fabric to the back of the board. Finish by applying a grid of coordinating ribbon. If you wish, hot-glue decorative nailheads or beads where ribbons intersect.

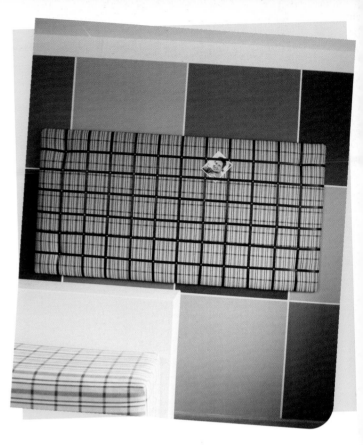

"I'm really thrilled how [the room] turned out," Doug says. "It's not originally the way I had envisioned it, but I always have Plan A and Plan B. That's part of the fun of it—being able to hit stumbling blocks and get over them. I like to show people how to achieve success when you are faced with challenges."

10 Must-Haves for the home office

1. **Storage, storage, and more storage.** No one ever complains about having too much storage. If you're fortunate enough to have a few empty shelves, fill the space with framed photos and decorative accessories.

2. **The right light.** Whether you're writing a novel or balancing a checkbook, you need pleasant overall illumination and adequate task lighting for the job.

3. **A generous work surface.** Even neatniks need room to spread out paperwork and supplies.

4. **A really great work chair.** Being comfortable allows your mind to focus on work rather than an aching back. Visit office supply and furniture stores and test a variety of chairs in order to find the one that fits you best. Be prepared to pay for quality and comfort.

5. **Welcoming ambience.** Paint the office your favorite color and fill it with mementos. You'll be amazed at how inviting it feels and how much more you enjoy working in the space.

6. **A computer.** In a high-tech world, who can work without one?

7. **Internet connections.** Whether you use your office to make quilts, oil paintings, or appointments, you'll likely need easy access to e-mail and the Internet.

8. **Plenty of outlets.** Tally up all your electronic gear, phones, and cable modems to see if you have enough connections for electric, cable, and phone service.

9. **Windows.** Arrange furniture to take advantage of a window view and add attractive exterior plantings and structures, such as an arbor, to enhance the scenery. If your office lacks a window, create your dream view by painting a faux window. Use an opaque projector to cast an image on the wall—the beach perhaps? Then trace and paint.

10. **Visitor chairs.** Clients, kids, and family pets will feel welcome when offered a comfortable place to sit.

◀ Adjustable shelves make display areas like this one even more functional. To keep items organized, outfit shelves with inexpensive colorful cardboard file boxes (available at office supply stores) and woven baskets. Then fill in (but not too much!) with books and a few favorite decorative pieces for color and shapely interest.

mdf
or plywood?

How do you decide whether to construct a project from MDF or plywood? Take a cue from the *Trading Spaces* designers and save veneered plywood for projects you plan to stain. Use lower-cost MDF whenever you want to have a painted finish.

▸ **PLYWOOD** is made up of veneer layers; it's very strong because the grain in each layer runs perpendicular to the grain of adjacent layers. For a smooth, attractive outside layer, choose A-rated plywood. Birch plywood is popular because its grain is light and the surface looks good whether it's painted or stained. Oak or birch plywood costs $30–$35 for a ½-inch-thick 4×8-foot sheet.

▸ **MDF** comes in 4×8-foot sheets measuring ½- or ¾-inch thick. Cut MDF as you would plywood and finish the edges with a router, if you wish. Join the pieces with straight-shank sheet metal screws, which are less likely to pull loose. Make screw holes at least 1 inch from the edge of the sheet and 2 inches in from the corners. To avoid splitting the panel, drill pilot holes and space screws at least 6 inches apart.

▸ **WHEN BUILDING PROJECTS WITH MDF,** keep in mind that this material is often heavier than plywood. You may need someone to help you maneuver pieces into place and to transport assembled projects.

▸ **WHEN CUTTING MDF OR PLYWOOD,** always wear safety goggles and gloves to avoid splinters and flying pieces.

versatile
storage bench

Think of all the things in your home that may need homes of their own. Boots, scarves, and mittens? Blankets or extra bed pillows? How about board games, cards, and video games? Does your child need a place to quickly put away toys?

A rolling storage bench like this can store any and all of those things. This project transforms an ordinary wood storage chest or toy box into a rolling catchall with a chic industrial-style metal top and casters. To find a suitable chest, shop at home centers and stores that sell unfinished furniture or look online and in catalogs. If young children will use the storage bench, outfit it with a hinge that locks into the open position to prevent the lid from coming down unexpectedly.

A.

B.

C.

what you need

Materials
Small storage chest
Sandpaper
1×4 board, 4 feet long
Wood glue
4 industrial-style wheels
   with a screw base (2 with
   locks and 2 without locks;
   choose a size that suits
   the size of the chest;
   these are 3-inch wheels)
Metal flashing, wide
   enough to cover chest
   lid (available at home
   centers in the ventilation
   or roofing departments)
Painter's tape
Flathead galvanized screws
Narrow corner molding
Acrylic paint: black
Small finishing brads
Wood filler

Tools
Jigsaw or saber saw
Offset tin snips
Fine-tipped marker
Tape measure
Awl
Hammer
Drill with screwdriver bit
Miter saw or handsaw
   with miter box
Paintbrush

1. **Cut off the legs of the chest,** if it has any. Sand smooth the places where legs were removed. To stabilize the wheels and protect the chest bottom, cut eight 3¾-inch-long blocks from the 1×4.

2. **Glue a block** in each inside corner of the chest (see Photo A).

3. **When the glue dries,** glue a second set of blocks on the exterior bottom of the chest, directly beneath the interior blocks. (If the lower edge of the chest has any lip, the extra blocks will make the wheels more visible.)

4. **Measure the top** of the chest. Mark the measurements onto the flashing and draw lines with the fine-tipped marker to outline a pattern for the chest top. Use the offset tin snips to cut out the new top (see Photo B). Note: Regular snips may also be used; offset snips give a more even and accurate cut and keep the edges from curling.

5. **Place the flashing** on the chest lid. Determine how many screws you want to place in the top in a grid pattern. Outlining the desired grid pattern,

tape the flashing to the top of the chest as shown. Mark the placement of the screws on the tape. Use an awl to make a hole for the first screw (see Photo C). Peel back the tape and insert the screw. Repeat for the remaining screws, removing the tape before inserting each screw.

6. **Measure the outside edge** of the lid and mark the corner molding pieces to fit the lid. Cut the pieces, mitering the corners. Paint the strips black. Nail the strips to the side edges of the lid, covering the edges of the metal and forming a frame around the flashing. Fill the nail holes with wood filler and touch up with paint.

7. **Turn the chest upside down** on a protected surface and position the wheels on the corner blocks. Screw the wheels in place (see Photo D).

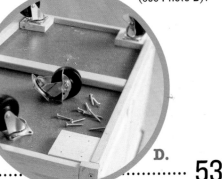

D.

Asian confluence

Entertaining idea
Plain wood shelves become classic and elegant when dressed in black and augmented with doors that keep the television under wraps.

Wicker works
To play up the Asian elements in the room and make the space both sophisticated and casual, wicker furniture enters the mix.

DESIGNED BY VERN

Merging disparate furnishings is a common design dilemma often occurring when two households come together. Vern undertakes the challenge in this generously sized family room and achieves beautiful results. A few additional wicker pieces, a sea-grass rug, and black accents play key roles in shaping an international flavor that's unified, stylish, and affordable.

Friendly neutrals
Sandstone color warms the walls and establishes a backdrop designed to unify a variety of furniture styles.

Hanging around
When you have a small budget and need to make a big impact, large mirrors can deliver the punch. Look for overscale models with high style, such as this dramatic round example, at import and discount furniture and decorating stores.

Black magic
Dashes of black always make a room seem more pulled together. Painting the existing coffee table black ties it to the entertainment center, the mirror, and the fabric edge on the rug.

Floor show
Bold, old carpeting was given the deep six in this family room in favor of wall-to-wall carpet squares. The subtle tone of the carpet will accommodate changes in furnishings and color schemes.

Textural addition
The natural fibers of a sea-grass rug effortlessly initiate the style shift in this room, adding character that's relaxed and Asian-inspired.

▶before

A room of mismatched furnishings, an expanse of dreadful flooring, and a microscopic $1,000 budget might sound like the beginnings of a decorating disaster. However, in this family room Vern cleverly finds a way through all these challenges by adapting existing furniture, giving it updated style and new uses. He also adds a few new pieces of furniture and finds a low-cost carpet product that's attractive and easy to install.

After pulling up the old carpet, Vern lays neutral-tone carpet tiles with unusual wavy-cut sides. No stapling is necessary; the tiles interlock for fast installation. Defending his choice of a subtle

▶Pennsylvania: Stump Drive

This extra large family room presents the look of two spaces. A wide array of furniture styles makes the room seem more disjointed. The homeowners hope that Vern can combine all their different styles into a cool and cohesive package. Though they're not afraid of color, they want the new design to blend with the other rooms in the house.

▶Floor-to-ceiling velvet curtains add drama to the room. To give your window treatments more style for a small investment, install plastic or painted-wood hardware designed for windows. These versatile adornments are available at home centers and discount stores. Choose basic, classic designs, avoiding pieces that are too frilly.

carpet color, Vern says, "With a color like this, you could have [any color sofa you want]. When it comes to putting down major things like carpet, this isn't something that you will want to change every year or so. This is something that you make an investment in so it allows you that flexibility to do whatever you want in the room."

In keeping with the same philosophy, Vern refreshes the walls with sandstone color and dresses an existing sofa in a neutral slipcover to accommodate colorful pillows.

Because the room serves as a space for quiet family evenings and for get-togethers with friends, it needs to be both casual and

money crunch $

▶ double-duty storage

By including the woven baskets in the living room, *left,* Vern gave the setting more textural interest, more hidden storage for small items, and more tabletop surfaces. Consider these other attractive storage options that can raise the style status of your rooms:

▶ **ARMOIRES.** Watch episodes of *Trading Spaces,* and you'll soon learn that armoire designs are as plentiful as discarded ceiling fans. An armoire can have plain or fancy doors and hardware. Inside, it may be outfitted with shelves, bins, cubbies, drawers, slots, or a closet pole—the options are almost unlimited. Use an armoire to store clothing or books, to house media equipment, or to accommodate a beverage or wine bar.

▶ **OTTOMANS.** Check catalogs, furniture stores, and online sources for ottomans with hidden storage. Use a storage ottoman to stash board games, books, or blankets and pillows.

▶ **CUBES.** Arrange storage and display cubes in creative configurations. Stack them symmetrically, asymmetrically, or in a row, a tall tower, or a stair-step design. Then use the cubes to corral books, collections, a small stereo, or colorful file boxes and woven baskets.

▶ **BENCHES.** Wooden benches or toy chests with lift-up lids offer good storage capacity and a place to sit. Top the lid with a cushion or take on the project on page 52, which transforms an ordinary wooden toy chest into a stylish rolling storage piece. The metal top looks good and is a practical surface for potted plants or drinks—no coasters required!

◄Pillows are an inexpensive way to make a quick color change in a room. These pillows mimic the texture of wicker pieces in the room.

10 Must-Haves for the living room

1. **Furniture you can actually sit on.** That too-good-to-touch stuff your mama chased you off of is a thing of the past. Today's upholstered pieces need to look good and feel even better.

2. **An entertainment center.** The TV and stereo equipment can actually look pretty stylish if you find (or design and construct) a storage system that complements your decor.

3. **Task and ambient lighting.** The right combination of lighting fixtures sets the mood and enables you to read, work, and entertain comfortably.

4. **A welcoming hearth.** A lovely hearth and a glowing fire warm the ambience of the room and give the space an unmistakably homey feel. If your home doesn't have a hearth, fake the effect by installing a new or vintage fireplace surround and filling a false firebox with candles and a mirrored backing.

5. **Display space.** There is no better way to convey the personalities of household members than to display the collectibles you cherish most.

6. **Storage.** You have to stash those piles of newspapers and board games somewhere.

7. **One or two ottomans.** This versatile piece of furniture works great for extra seating and can double as a snack tray or game table.

8. **Small occasional tables.** Where an ottoman won't fit, a 10-inch round table will, and it can hold necessities such as coffee cups and paperbacks and niceties such as framed photos and votive candles.

9. **Armloads of throw pillows.** These cushy wonders make even the homeliest sofa look better.

10. **Artwork.** If your budget doesn't allow you to buy a few framed pieces, make your own.

beautiful. For beauty Vern focuses his efforts on making the furnishings more cohesive. Some of the existing furniture, such as a coffee table with Oriental influences, serves as a springboard for expanding an Asian theme to the entire room. Existing bookcases stay in the room too, sporting new coats of black paint that provide a visual thread between the shelves and the coffee table. A new sea-grass rug solidifies the look with its black cloth edge.

Vern enhances the casual mood of the space by adding more texture, including MDF planters surfaced in sisal and tropical houseplants that enliven the space with green.

To finish the room and address the homeowners' wishes for more seating, Vern brings in a pair of wicker chaises. The seating is ideal for relaxing in front of the television, which now hides behind doors newly attached to the center bookcase. Other wicker pieces, such as storage cubes and baskets, round out the tactile treasures that make this room feel unified and complete.

"By reusing the existing furniture," Vern says, "we were able to afford the flooring and do some of the other projects."

paint

Purchasing quality paint is one of the best ways to ensure a successful outcome for any decorating project. Unfortunately, you can't assess the quality of paint by reading the label on the can or even by stirring the paint.

To ensure quality, purchase the top-of-the-line paint within your favorite manufacturer's line of products. Unless you're lucky enough to hit a paint sale, you'll likely purchase the most expensive paint in the line. The ingredients in these more expensive products are higher-quality, so the paint almost always outperforms ordinary-grade paint products. Here are some of the advantages of high-end paints:

▹ They are easier to apply.

▹ They have better hiding characteristics and often require fewer coats.

▹ They create a washable, more durable finish.

▹ They maintain their color and sheen better over time, so your paint job will look fresh longer.

▹ They contain more quality-enhancing additives, such as mildew and mold inhibitors.

Although you may spend more up front, painting with a top-quality paint will likely cut down the number of required coats and add years to the life of the paint job, ultimately saving you labor and material costs in years to come.

A top-quality paint job used to require an oil-base enamel paint. Now latex enamel paints are as durable as oil-base paints and are less likely to yellow over time. Also, latex paints can be easily cleaned off tools with mild soap and water.

Generally, finishes that have a sheen are more durable than flat finishes. If possible choose an eggshell, satin, or glossy finish for your project rather than a flat finish. Eggshell or satin finishes work well on walls; semigloss paints are ideal for woodwork, doors, and cabinets.

◀ Pillows make this wicker chaise more comfy. Though the chaise and its matching companion (out of view) are pricey, they're worth the splurge because they're striking enough to make the whole room seem special.

▲ Though the substantial planters look expensive, MDF construction and sisal doormats glued to the sides make them affordable. The doormats cost only $1 each. The black trim is painted strips of MDF. Because the plants are housed in smaller containers set inside the MDF boxes, replacing the greenery is an easy, no-mess job.

fashionable floorcloth

Because you decide on the design and colors, a painted floorcloth is a great way to gain a custom rug in almost any size or shape you need. This project is painted on a linoleum remnant. The rigidity of linoleum ensures a wrinkle-free floor covering. In addition, the material is durable, and the painted and sealed surface is easy to vacuum and clean. Most home centers have 6×9-foot remnants available for as little as $15; you may be able to find smaller remnants for free from someone finishing up a remodeling project.

A.

B.

what you need

Materials

Linoleum remnant of
  the desired size
Latex primer
Acrylic or crafts paints:
  sage green, royal blue,
  light sky blue, olive
  green, Kelly green,
  dark mulberry, white,
  yellow, red
1-inch-wide painter's tape
Stencils in the desired
  designs (purchased or
  homemade)
Clear water-base
  poly-acrylic sealer
Rubber cement

Tools

Measuring tape
Extralong straightedge
  and T-square
Utility knife with
  new blade
Self-healing cutting mat
Drop cloth
Roller or wide paintbrush
  to apply primer
Angled trim paintbrush
Stencil brush

1. Cut the remnant to the desired size. Check that all four corners are square by using a pencil and a T square; use a utility knife and a long straightedge to cut the sides evenly. Cut on an appropriate surface, such as a self-healing cutting mat, and slide the remnant across the mat as you cut. If you wish, cut the corners at an angle, as shown in the photograph of the finished floorcloth.

2. Flip the linoleum so the wrong side is up (see Photo A). This is the side you'll paint. (The printed side of the linoleum will be the bottom of the floorcloth.) Prime the surface of the floorcloth, using a good-quality primer and a small roller or brush. If you use a small roller, dip it directly into the primer to eliminate the need for a roller tray and extra cleanup. Let dry.

3. To create the painterly background for the floorcloth, you'll need an angled trim paintbrush and acrylic or crafts paints in sage green, royal blue, light sky blue, olive green, and Kelly green. Position the remnant on the drop cloth. Dip the brush in sage green first and begin painting in a crosshatching motion, starting at the

center of the floorcloth and working outward to the edges (see Photo B). Dip the brush in royal blue and apply in random crosshatch strokes, lightly blending as you work. Apply sage green again in the same manner, then apply light sky blue. Alternate sage green and other colors until you use all the hues. Let dry overnight.

4. Measure and mark the stripe design, using a pencil and the longest straightedge you can find. The first stripe is 4 inches in from the edge; the stripes are 1 inch apart. Each stripe measures 1 inch wide, and the stripes overlap at each corner. Use painter's tape to mask off the edges of the stripes on two opposite edges of the floorcloth. Press the edges of the tape down with your fingernail to prevent the paint from bleeding underneath. Paint the stripes dark mulberry (see Photo C). Remove the tape, then let the paint dry thoroughly before repeating the striping steps on the remaining two opposite sides of the floorcloth. Remove the tape after painting these stripes and let the stripes dry thoroughly.

5. Stencil designs onto the middle section of the floorcloth (see Photo D). Use the same colors as you did for the background, as well as white, yellow, red, and dark mulberry paint. When stenciling use as little paint as possible to prevent the paint from bleeding underneath the stencil.

6. Seal the surface of the floorcloth with three coats of clear water-base poly-acrylic sealer. Let the sealer dry between coats.

7. To prevent the floorcloth from sliding on the floor, flip it over onto a protected surface. Brush rubber cement onto the underside of the floorcloth (which was once the top of the linoleum). Let dry and position the floorcloth where desired. The rubber cement remains tacky for a better grip yet doesn't harm flooring.

D.

C.

opportunity knocks

DESIGNED BY CHRISTI

Easy green
This soft, soothing green is easy on the eyes and oh-so-relaxing for the family who gathers here.

Pretty patches
A patchwork of solid fabrics interspersed with black and white toile makes these pillows a lively standout against the neutral slipcovered couch.

Goodbye plaid
Who would ever guess this sofa was once plaid? A new more fashionable slipcover erases the memory and gives the sofa a fresh start—for a fraction of the cost of a new piece.

Old or new?
Paint and sandpaper can give new, unfinished furniture and thrift store finds vintage appeal. Brush on paint color, let dry, and then gently sand edges to instantly age the piece. This side table, part of the original decor, aged gracefully during the makeover.

Sticky business
Using white glue to stick on photographs (actually color copies) of friends and family makes changing the display easy. For variation, use photos of vacations or pets.

Knob appeal
This crystal doorknob sparkles like jewelry. If you find a door with a down-and-out knob, change the knob to something more attractive. Reproduction styles are readily available at home centers, often at affordable prices.

Knock, knock
Think differently when designing your new space. This salvaged door hangs horizontally on the wall—instant artwork!

Sometimes, saving money involves recognizing bargains and taking advantage of them—even when you're not sure how you'll use your treasure. This living room gains vintage character when Christi incorporates an unexpected find: two salvaged doors that open up new decorating possibilities.

before

▶ Pennsylvania: Stump Drive

The cow borders can "moo-ve" out; still, Christi needs to steer attention away from a permanent feature: the narrowness of the room. The fireplace is a natural focal point, and Christi has a clever plan to create another attention-grabber on an adjacent wall. A family of six lives here, so the room needs abundant seating and lots of comfort too.

From the Designers

▶ CHRISTI PROCTOR

Q In addition to the home furnishings and accessories department at discount stores, what other departments do you visit for cool decorating materials and ideas?

A I always hit the candle departments close to the stationery department. That's where they always seem to hide the good candle sconces and candlelight fixtures.

Q What is one item or aspect of a room that is worth splurging on?

A Always fabrics. You can make a sofa pop with an extraspecial fabric on a throw pillow.

1. **Palatable colors.** Reds and pinks increase the appetite; yellows and oranges enliven the mood.
2. **Flexible seating.** Invest in a table that comfortably seats as many as 10 or as few as 2.
3. **Comfortable seating.** Cushioned chairs encourage guests to linger.
4. **Flexible lighting.** Installing a dimmer switch lets you match the lighting to the setting—whether it's a birthday party for 4-year-olds or a romantic dinner for two.
5. **Light-controlling window treatments.** Carefully chosen window treatments can act as a dimmer switch for sunlight.
6. **Buffet service.** A side table, hutch, or bar lets you spend more time entertaining and less time waiting tables.
7. **Combination storage and display space.** Display good dishes without filling up kitchen cabinets.
8. **Terrific table toppers.** Make the setting look as good as possible.
9. **Wall art.** The walls in the dining room are viewed for long periods of time, so why not put your money where the mouths are?
10. **Lots of candles.** Stack them on trays to create an impromptu centerpiece.

◄ Painting the mantel off-white allows it to stand out against the green walls—a fast, cost-efficient way to create a focal point.

The members of the household—a family of six—use this family room for everything. They ask Christi for an updated look, plenty of style, and a nice dose of color. To increase the functionality of the room, which adjoins the kitchen, Christi asks Carter to lengthen a half-wall between the two spaces. Here, she decides to creatively employ a salvaged door as a countertop between the two rooms. A second salvaged door becomes custom artwork above one of the sofas; Christi opts to hang the door horizontally and use the recessed panels as frames for family photos. Both existing sofas, which were upholstered in plaid fabric, switch into contemporary dress—touchable, soft brushed twill that Christi discovered at the closeout price of $2 per yard. A coffee table, side tables, and the salvaged doors gain vintage appeal from an easy and inexpensive painted finish that's sanded on the edges for a weathered look.

▲ Salvage can often be retrofitted to suit your cause; it's worth the effort if the piece is a bargain. Here, Carter added MDF to the end of a door to make it long enough to serve as a countertop. Paint hides the resulting seam.

◄ Flea markets and garage sales are good sources for boxes full of fun, low-cost finds. Watch for items that can double as hangers for window treatments, such as these doorknobs. Coat hooks, cabinet knobs, and even billiard balls are other playful options.

make over your dining room

before

$100

Many people move into a new home with a formal dining room, only to realize that they don't own a stick of dining room furniture. Although decorating a blank slate can be fun, a barren budget is much less entertaining. Fortunately, if you have $100, your dining room can be made into a great place to entertain friends and family. Build on the look as decorating dollars become available. This dining space, which was inspired by the show, celebrates books and Asian-inspired elements.

▶$100 budget breakdown

paint for walls (1 gallon)	$12
solid-core oak door	$50
paint and polyurethane for door	$10
pillows (4)	$20
candles	$4
assorted paper products	$7
TOTAL	**$103**

▶**RICHLY RED.** Remove mismatched wall art and blah vertical blinds. (This dining room looks out onto a screen porch, so no treatments are necessary.) Paint two walls tomato bisque red.

▶**EASY, EXOTIC TABLE.** Stain and paint a solid-core oak door, then rest the door on four stacks of colorful books for a casual dining surface.

▶**SINK-IN SEATING.** Scatter pillows around the table. Create pillowcases for old pillows from scraps of spicy-colored material.

▶**FESTIVE TABLETOP.** Purchase boldly colored paper plates and napkins and plastic utensils—no basic white! Use large pieces of color construction paper as place mats.

▶**PLANT POWER.** Spotlight a single gorgeous flower or houseplant by displaying it on a stack of books at one end of a long table (such as the beautiful bonsai tree that appears here).

▶**WARM GLOW.** Focus attention around the table by turning off the outdated light fixture and clustering assorted candles.

▶ $500 budget breakdown

mountable aluminum table legs (4)	$109
matchstick blinds (2)	$24
pre-stretched artist's canvases (6)	$22
acrylic artist's paints for canvases	$5
pine shelving units for buffet base (2)	$36
red velvet to skirt buffet (4 yards)	$24
aspen plank (to top buffet)	$21
metal/plastic folding chairs (4)	$80
cotton fabric for table runner (3 yards)	$8
dark red wall paint (I quart)	$8
valance hardware kits (2)	$6
velvet for valances	$10
molding	$6
fabric to cover light fixture	$5
centerpiece	$9
wineglasses (4)	$16
ceramic plates (4)	$16
cloth napkins (4)	$8
napkin rings (4)	$8
TOTAL	**$421**
PREVIOUS TOTAL	**$103**
NEW TOTAL	**$524**

$500

▶**LEG UP.** Pair sleek metal table legs with the stained door for a full-height dining table. Sets of prefabricated metal and wood legs are available in many sizes and finishes at office furniture stores and home centers and from online retailers. Installation requires only a drill and bits.

▶**SLEEK SEATING.** Select a quartet of modern metal or plastic folding chairs to use as temporary dining chairs. When more permanent chairs replace these, the folding chairs can still be used for larger dining parties and celebrations.

▶**WINDOW WONDER.** Hang inexpensive, unlined matchstick blinds on windows.

▶**FRAMED ART.** Hang six color-block canvases that share one wide painted-on frame as shown. Use painter's tape to make crisp lines.

▶**UPGRADE TABLE SERVICE.** Swap out paper plates and napkins for black-glazed ceramic and cloth. Clear glass goblets and beaded napkin rings round out the table.

▶**BASIC BUFFET.** Create a base to serve meals from and display treasures by topping two bookcases with an aspen plank and skirting the whole unit in fabric.

▶**STRIP STYLE.** Introduce coordinating color by painting a strip of dark red behind the server and fashioning a table runner from several yards of inexpensive fabric.

▶**DELIGHTFUL LIGHTING.** Wrap an unsightly light fixture in sheer fabric for a softened glow. Stick an assortment of tapers in a container filled with sand for an easy, versatile centerpiece, *above.*

$1,000

UPGRADE SEATING. Replace folding chairs with four permanent chairs made of wicker, iron, and bamboo. Toss a colorful pillow on each seat for additional luxury and comfort.

DISPLAY HEYDAY (1). Hang two open shelves above the buffet base to create a serving hutch. Display dishware, collections, and plants.

GET GROUNDED. Place a large rug under the table to ground the dining area and its furniture. This rug is office carpet that can be replaced quickly and inexpensively when it becomes soiled or styles change.

OLD TO NEW. Convert old chandelier globes to votive candleholders. Group globes together for maximum impact.

WOVEN WONDER (2). Create textural custom art by weaving satin ribbons of varying widths through a large matchstick blind.

LIGHT ON. Create a custom light fixture by running inexpensive lightbulb kits (available at most hardware stores, home centers, and discount retailers) through metal buckets that have been drilled through the bottom. Hardwire the lamp cords directly to the ceiling receptacle rather than trailing cords over the ceiling and wall. Cap the ceiling receptacle with a wooden frame wrapped in matchstick blinds.

ADD LIFE. Two types of grass and a bowl of nectarines join the bonsai tree and other colorful accents on the serving hutch.

▶$1,000 budget breakdown

Upgraded metal/wicker dining chairs (4)	$276
Identical centerpiece (with new candles for both)	$12
Matchstick blind for wall art	$18
Ribbon for wall art	$7
Wall shelves (2)	$30
Wooden frame for light fixture	$7
Buckets for light fixture (3)	$15
Light-wiring kits and other electrical components	$34
Plants	$15
Set of banded boxes	$7
Rug	$18
Champagne bucket	$5
Silverware for 4	$30
TOTAL	**$474**
PREVIOUS TOTAL	**$519**
ROOM TOTAL	**$993**

The velvet touch

The scheme is monochromatic yet never boring. Contrasting fabric textures, such as these sexy velvet draperies, keep the look exciting.

Shapely sofa

A flowing asymmetrical back makes this sofa a work of art. The piece sets a playful tone.

Snake charmer

Hot pink python-print vinyl introduces a touch of Hollywood glam. Real leather would gobble up the budget; look-alikes such as this are less expensive and more fun.

Sparkle plenty

Another dash of glitz shows up in the form of pillows made from sparkly fabric.

Let it snow

A clear coffee table invites a tongue-in-cheek display of snow globes the owners collect. Hildi added the globe featuring the Eiffel Tower.

Break time

An ultrafluffy white rug provides visual relief from all the color and comforts the toes too.

'Wow!' color

There are times when you simply have to make the statement clear: You love color and plenty of it. Here, Hildi has fun with one color, drenching the room in subtly shifting magenta.

mom's lipstick palace

DESIGNED BY HILDI

"Take a risk," the owners said. So, of course, Hildi was delighted to oblige with bold magenta hey-look-at-me color and a shapely, sexy sofa wrapped in pink python-print vinyl. Lights tucked into the toe-kick of the sofa make the furniture appear to be floating. Toss in a few sparkles and some decadent velvet, and you know this isn't your mama's sitting room.

Lights! Action!

Ceramic lights create the illusion that the sofa is floating. How do they do that?

▶before

▶Philadelphia: Cresheim Road

The coffee table is kind of cool; the futon and desk are standard fare. White walls and a white rug are ultrabland. The homeowners say they are definitely ready for some style-on-the-edge, and who better than Hildi to deliver it? Though the painted floor is a nice touch, Hildi has something more happenin' in mind.

t started as a plain white office space that the owners considered "really bland." Hildi hears their plea: "We would love to see [the designer] take a risk and make the room something exciting. Loosen up and go nuts."

The office space is located off the master bedroom, so Hildi decides that the room can double as a sitting room and office. Whether the room began with the flashy pink python-print vinyl or the deep magenta paint labeled "Mom's Lipstick" is anyone's guess; regardless, the final design is nothing short of spectacular.

Hildi sets the stage by generously applying magenta paint to nearly every paintable surface, including the walls, trim, doors, windows, and ceiling. The showstopping pink python-print vinyl makes its debut as upholstery fabric on a custom-built sofa. Of course, this is more than a mere sofa; it's an II-foot-long eye-popping work of art with an undulating back that was achieved by linking pieces of MDF with flat iron brackets. Hildi cuts out the noteworthy sofa back herself, using a jigsaw. The sofa sits on a black-painted MDF base. Creating a slight overhang with the seat portion allows ceramic light fixtures to slip into the recess. When these lights are on, the sofa appears to float.

Floor-to-ceiling magenta velvet draperies and a curved chair covered to match introduce some touchable fabrics to the space.

Together the painted surfaces and the vinyl and velvet fabrics compose a monochromatic scheme that makes the room dramatic and moody as well as wonderfully enveloping. (If you've never designed or decorated a monochromatic room, take this easy approach: Select a color that shows up in every department of a department store. Buy items in varying shades of the same color, choosing different textural finishes to keep the look interesting.)

Adding crisp white to a monochromatic room typically makes the color of choice seem even more intense. At the same time, the

▲ Ready-to-assemble, or RTA, seating, such as the chair shown here, often costs less than furniture assembled by the manufacturer. Hildi customized this piece with velvet fabric to match the draperies.

◄ A straight run of MDF forms a desk top that supports the homeowners' keyboard. Use a 2× cleat below the panel to support the desk top. (Screw down through the desk top into the cleat and check that the cleat is securely screwed to studs.) Paint the cleat the same color as the wall and it virtually disappears.

money crunch $

► low-cost seating

If building furniture from scratch goes beyond your skill set, check out these inexpensive seating alternatives:

► **THRIFT STORE FINDS.** Salvation Army, Goodwill, and scores of other outlets are secondhand heavens. Visit often to catch new goods as they arrive.

► **RTA.** Ready-to-assemble furnishings are often less expensive than the pieces you purchase already assembled. Look for RTAs in catalogs and online.

► **PILLOW TALK.** What's more cuddly and comfy than a giant stuffed floor pillow? Buy a bolt or two of bargain fabric and stitch pillow covers: Cut two same-size squares of fabric, stack the squares with right sides facing, and stitch together on three sides (or use iron-on hem tape to join the sides). Stuff the pillow with acrylic batting and hand-stitch the remaining edge closed (or use more iron-on hem tape).

► **COLLEGE KICKS.** Beanbags and butterfly chairs have moved out of the dorms and into established homes. Add extra seating with these affordable options. Butterfly chairs offer the added benefit of folding up for easy storage.

► **OTTOMAN EMPIRE.** Ottomans are less expensive than chairs and can function as additional seating when needed. Designed to prop up feet, ottomans are sometimes promoted to the position of coffee table.

◄ To buy a sofa like this you'd pay a princely sum. Make it yourself and you'll smile all the way to the bank. The lights, by the way, aren't really supporting the sofa; they rest beneath the lip. An MDF base, which is covered with foam, stands behind the light and plays the supporting role. Watch for closeout deals on fabulous fabrics, such as this fun python-print vinyl, and buy bolts you love when you find them. Stash them for a rainy day—you'll soon figure out a great way to put the fabric to work.

cool white offers visual relief. In this room, shelves and a desk top fashioned from MDF are more than functional—they add refreshing splashes of white.

Plants add a lively touch to the room too. Though the patio daisies look terrific and will last for at least a few months, you may want to invest in tall silk flowering plants for a similar vertical look, long-lasting beauty, and no maintenance.

For the floor, Hildi makes another unconventional choice: Using a spray adhesive she affixes 26-inch-square foam tiles to the subfloor. The floor feels fabulous under bare or stocking feet; heels are a no-no.

houseplants

Houseplants bring welcome color and life to a room for a small investment. If you choose the right ones for your environment, they can remain healthy and attractive with very little maintenance. To stay on-budget, choose small, fast-growing plants such as a philodendron or pothos; with a little tender loving care, these plants can double in size within three months. For added color and design dash, paint the clay pots to match your decor.

▶ **POTHOS.** This easy-to-maintain plant can grow in most light conditions; however, it requires bright, filtered light to maintain its color variations. Allow the soil to dry 2 inches below the surface before watering.

▶ **CACTUS.** This desert transplant can survive in less-than-ideal conditions such as a cool foyer or a cool or warm sunroom. Pot in a cactus soil mix and allow the soil to dry almost entirely before watering.

▶ **FIDDLE-LEAF FIG.** This plant grows to be 4 or 5 feet tall and can be pruned to shape. The plant has a tendency to become root-bound, so plan to repot once or twice a year. The large leaves attract dust, so you'll need to wipe them down with a damp cloth.

▶ **PHILODENDRON.** Easy maintenance makes this houseplant a favorite. Like the pothos, the philodendron grows best in bright, filtered light. Let the soil dry 2 inches below the surface between waterings. Overwatering causes the leaves to yellow; underwatering causes the leaves to turn brown and fall off.

▶ **CROTON.** To keep the leaves of this popular plant in full color, place the plant in a window that gets bright light. Crotons like warm, moist conditions and thrive in steamy, window-filled bathrooms.

▶ **EVERLASTING HOUSEPLANTS.** OK, these aren't really live plants. However, the latest offerings in the everlasting plant market look like the real thing, and some of the better versions even feel like live plants. If you find it difficult to water regularly or suffer from plant-related allergies, check local florist shops for some of these nearly real renditions.

To finish the room a few black and white photos are mounted on white mats with clear frames. When the dust settles, everyone—including Hildi—is delighted with the results. "I really wanted to make a difference in the room," she says. "And they wanted something different. They wanted outrageous."

Mom would be proud.

▲ Though MDF is weighty stuff, it's often less expensive than plywood and can be routed on the edges for a stylish finish, as the details on these shelves illustrate. A coat of white paint makes the unit pop against the magenta walls.

Under $30

what you need

Materials

Latex paint for base coat
Graph paper
Silver-composition leaf
 (1 package of twenty-
 five 5½-inch squares)
Cardboard template with
 a 5½-inch-square opening
Spray adhesive formulated
 for metallic leaf
Waxed paper

Tools

Paint roller
Carpenter's level
Long straightedge
Pencil

one 'wow' wall

S ilver-composition leaf is an inexpensive product that always
makes a powerful visual impact. For this project, use the
sheets right out of the package—no trimming required—to
create a striking wall with graphic beauty. Choose any
background color, keeping in mind that dark hues provide
dramatic contrast with the pale glimmer of the metallic leaf.
When undertaking this project, expect less-than-perfect
squares—that's part of the charm of the look.

1. **Paint the wall** with base coat color and let dry overnight.

2. **Plan the positions for** the silver-leaf squares and plot these locations on a sheet of graph paper before you start working on the wall. In this instance, one square on the graph paper equals 6 inches on the wall; one filled-in square represents one sheet of silver leaf. Draw the height and width of the wall on the graph paper and shade in the locations of the silver-leaf squares. In this bedroom, the silver-leaf squares are spaced 18 inches apart, from side to side and top to bottom. (So on the graph paper, you would leave three empty squares between shaded squares.)

3. **Mark the wall with a grid** of right angles to indicate the position of each silver-leaf square. Rather than mark the entire square, mark only the upper right-hand corners to limit the amount of pencil marks on the painted wall. Use a level to check that lines are plumb and level, and measure carefully (see Photo A). If you make an error, paint wall color over the error rather than using a pencil eraser to attempt to remove the mark.

4. **Prepare the square spaces** to accept the silver-leaf sheets by holding the cardboard template over each proposed square location (placing the right-hand corner of the template opening at the right-hand corner you've marked on the wall). Spray metallic-leaf adhesive through the template opening (see Photo B). Lift away the template to reveal the shiny square of adhesive; let dry until tacky—about 30 to

A.

B.

C.

60 minutes—while you repeat this adhesive-spraying process for the other squares.

5. **Place silver-leaf squares** over the tacky squares. Silver-leaf squares are delicate to handle and require a still room without a lot of activity or wind blowing through it. Before approaching the wall with a square, experiment with a square on scrap paper. For the best handling, make a sandwich—a silver-leaf square between two squares of the tissue paper that lies between the leaves of the silver-leaf booklet. Tear the tissues out

of the booklet as you work, saving them for the next square. If one becomes sticky with adhesive, throw it away. With only a slight edge of the silver leaf extending from the tissue paper sandwich, hold the edge up to the top edge of a tacky square (see Photo C). Let the edge of the leaf square attach itself to the edge of the square marked on the wall. Then slowly release the tissue paper from the silver leaf and let the silver square drop loosely in place on the wall.

6. **Place a small sheet of waxed paper** over the silver-leaf square and rub the waxed paper with your hand to secure the silver leaf (see Photo D).

Note: Though no square is perfect, take care to position each one squarely on the wall. Fill holes with scraps of silver leaf; adhesive visible through gaps and cracks will hold them in place. If an error seems too great, paint over the spot, let dry thoroughly, and begin the application steps again.

D.

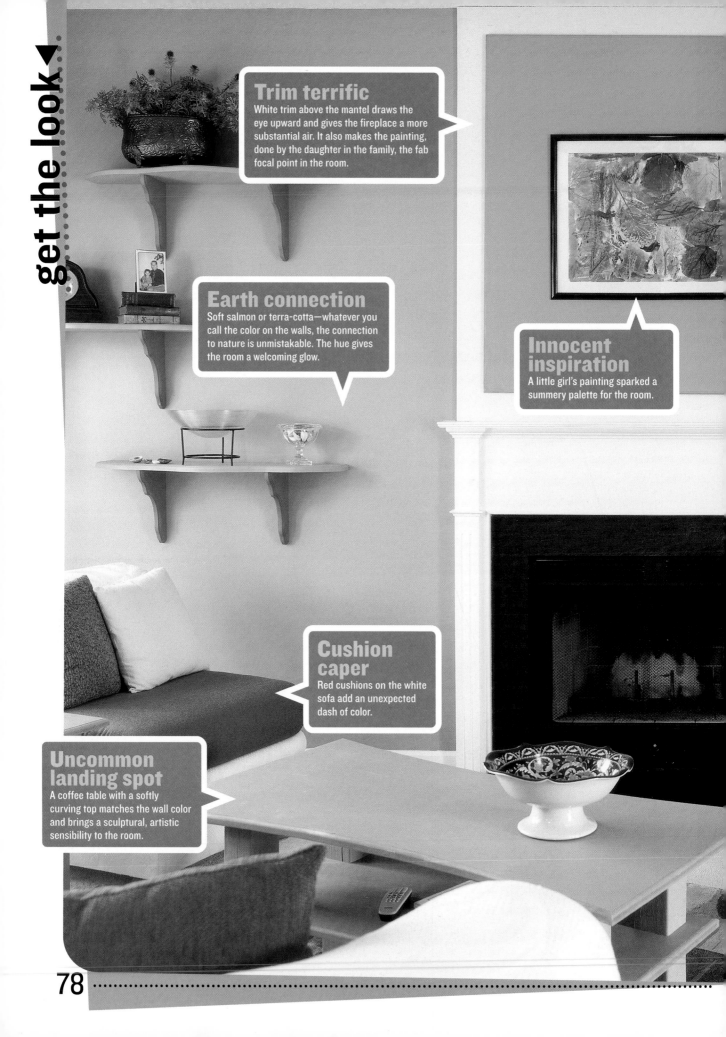

Trim terrific
White trim above the mantel draws the eye upward and gives the fireplace a more substantial air. It also makes the painting, done by the daughter in the family, the fab focal point in the room.

Earth connection
Soft salmon or terra-cotta—whatever you call the color on the walls, the connection to nature is unmistakable. The hue gives the room a welcoming glow.

Innocent inspiration
A little girl's painting sparked a summery palette for the room.

Cushion caper
Red cushions on the white sofa add an unexpected dash of color.

Uncommon landing spot
A coffee table with a softly curving top matches the wall color and brings a sculptural, artistic sensibility to the room.

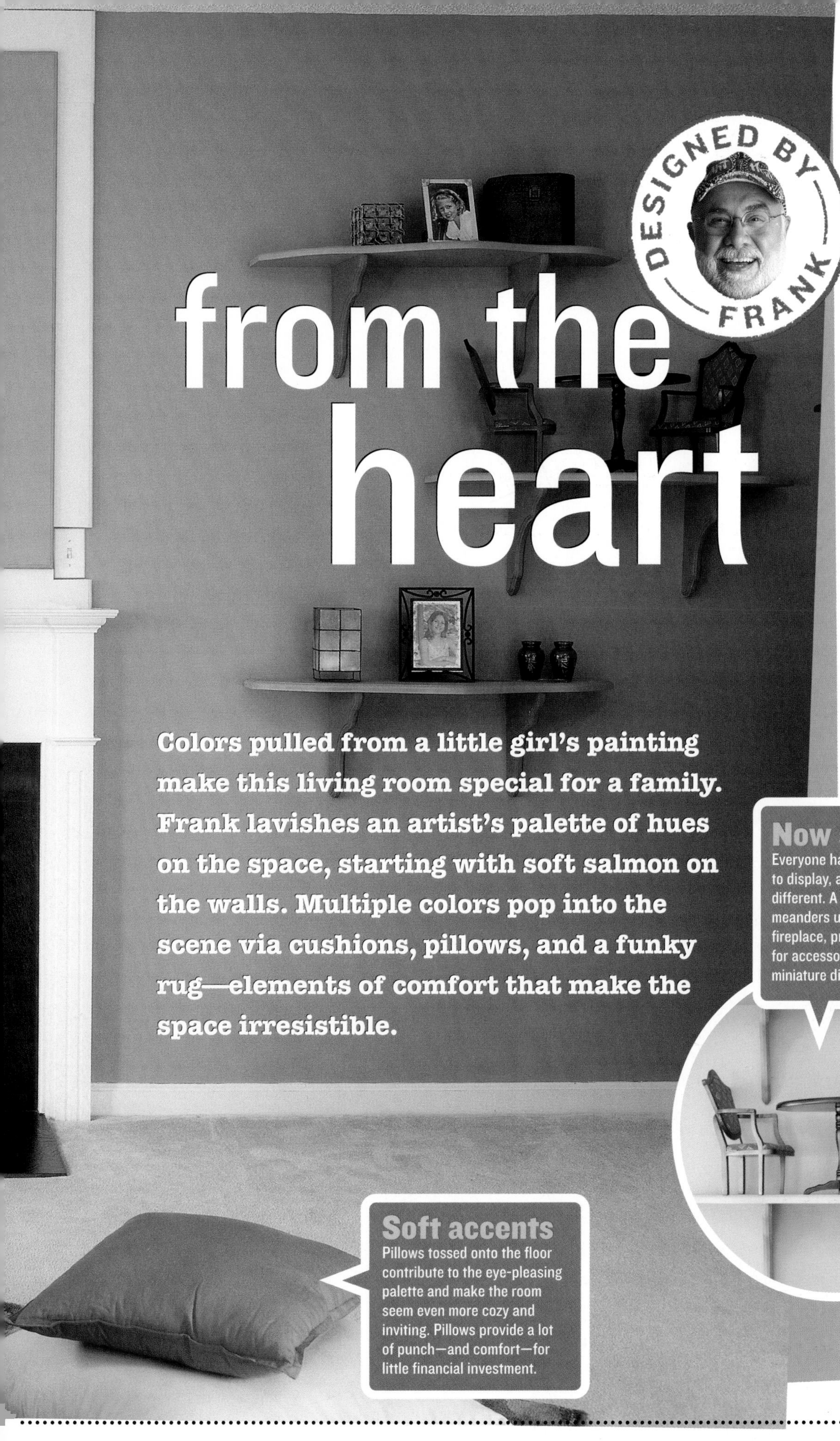

from the heart

Colors pulled from a little girl's painting make this living room special for a family. Frank lavishes an artist's palette of hues on the space, starting with soft salmon on the walls. Multiple colors pop into the scene via cushions, pillows, and a funky rug—elements of comfort that make the space irresistible.

Now see this

Everyone has a few treasures to display, and this family is no different. A trio of shelves meanders up each side of the fireplace, providing platforms for accessories such as this miniature dining set.

Soft accents

Pillows tossed onto the floor contribute to the eye-pleasing palette and make the room seem even more cozy and inviting. Pillows provide a lot of punch—and comfort—for little financial investment.

Like most family rooms, this one is used every day. The mom, dad, and daughter who live here eat popcorn, watch movies, play games—and even wrestle on the floor. The family tells Frank to add some fun and personality, and Frank thinks the daughter's charming painting is an ideal element to build on. Because the room is open to other spaces in the house, Frank wants the new color scheme to get along well with these adjacent areas. He introduces the wall color—soft salmon—to complement both the painting and some valances in an adjoining space.

The owners want to leave the original surround on the fireplace untouched, and Frank obliges. To improve the look, he adds white-painted trim above the fireplace and an MDF panel in the center to match the wall. The trim and panel function as a frame, drawing the eye to the focal-point painting. Trios of MDF shelves on each side of the fireplace offer display space and further establish this wall as the focal point of the room.

Putting the existing sofa and chair to work keeps the budget on course. The furnishings are in fairly good shape, so Frank merely covers the cushions with bold red fabric. He then paints the legs on the sofa and chair bright orange for unexpected accent color. Armloads of pillows introduce more color, and a few feature a playful pattern of free-form circles.

Furniture arrangement is fundamental in this makeover. Placed on the diagonal rather than against the walls, the pieces gather around a colorful, abstract-design rug. On the rug sits a new coffee table, custom-made from MDF mounted on 4×4 legs.

before

▶North Carolina: Love Valley Drive

This room has a pleasant-enough transitional style going on, and the white sofas have good lines. But the plain white fireplace and stained wood tables with Queen Anne-style legs steer the space into a realm that's much too serious for a room used for popcorn and movies. The homeowners say they're ready to kick up their heels and have a little fun with the look.

▶ superfunctional shelves

One of the finest ways to express your personality in a room is to show off your collections and books on shelves. Here are some things to keep in mind as you plan shelves for your space:

▶ **MATERIALS.** Home centers offer manufactured wood panels for under $15. Cut the panels to the desired size and then stain or paint the wood as desired. If you don't own a saw, ask the home center to cut the panels for you. MDF panels are an inexpensive alternative.

▶ **BRACKETS.** Decorative brackets are available through home centers, catalogs, and flea markets. Consider using creative alternatives too. Frank once used wire plant baskets to support a shelf.

▶ **SECURITY.** Check that your shelf can hold up under the weight of the objects you plan to display. Secure brackets to wall studs with screws or use appropriate hollow-wall anchors.

▶ **LOW-COST RESOURCES.** Check online and in catalogs for low-cost and stylish shelving options.

▲ "Use what you have" is the lesson in this family room. New cushion covers for the existing sofa and chair are inspired and colorful additions to the scheme. Pulling the pieces away from the walls and setting the arrangement on the diagonal costs nothing but offers high visual impact.

▶ Slipcovering only the couch cushion is less expensive than covering the entire thing—a smart choice when your sofa is in good shape but you're hankering for a fast change.

▶ ▶ Rugs today come in an enormous array of colors, patterns, and styles. Search online resources, catalogs, and discount stores for affordable renditions, such as this swirly modern design Frank selected.

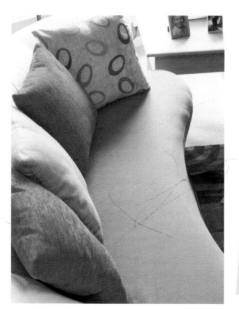

▲ The artwork beside the armoire cost practically nothing. By blowing through drinking straws, the neighbors scattered droplets of colored India ink into free-flowing streams across the paper.

The curved sides of the tabletop give the piece a subtle artistic turn that suits the room.

The neighbors make some inexpensive artwork by using drinking straws to blow streams of India ink around on paper. This forms abstract designs that Frank frames—a fitting artistic touch for a room inspired by a little girl's painting.

ladders and step stools

Whether you are hanging draperies, taking down a ceiling fan, or painting a wall cabinet, having the right stepladder or step stool on hand can make the job safer and easier.

▶ **ONE-STEP STOOLS** provide an additional reach of 9 to 14 inches, which means if you're 5 feet 5 inches tall, you'll be able to accessorize a shelf as high as 7 feet. Basic one-step stools start at about $15; fold-up and rolling models range from $20 to $100.

▶ **TWO-STEP STOOLS** add 16 to 18 inches to your reach. This much additional reach will allow almost anyone to grab dishes and ingredients off the top shelf in their kitchen cabinets. Superslim models fold to a depth of just 1 inch, so the stool can slip easily into a closet or pantry, between the washer and dryer, or next to the fridge. Prices range from $20 to $125.

▶ **THREE-STEP LADDERS** provide an additional reach of 24 to 29 inches, which means if you're of average height, you'll be able to change a lightbulb in a fixture as high as 8 feet. Look for a three-step ladder that has a high safety rail to help keep you balanced. Prices for three-step ladders range from $22 to $150.

▶ **FOR HOUSEHOLD PROJECTS** that require long periods of balance, such as ceiling painting and wallpapering, a taller stepladder offers a more comfortable reach and greater stability. Choose a ladder that brings you within 4 feet of the point you want to reach—3 feet is even better. For example, if you want to paint a 9-foot-high ceiling, choose a stepladder that is at least 5 feet tall; to paint a 10-foot-high ceiling, choose a stepladder that is at least 6 feet tall. Prices for 5- to 8-foot stepladders range from $35 to $450.

From the Designers

▶ FRANK BIELEC

Q If you had only $100 to pump up the style of a room, how would you spend your money?

A I would spend the money on paint and cleaning supplies. If you get all the furniture really clean and give the walls a fresh coat of paint, the whole room looks better. If you have any money left over, buy a couple of throw pillows.

Q What advice do you have for big-budget home decorators?

A Don't go buying a bunch of stuff for your room helter-skelter. I've never seen a U-Haul behind a hearse because you can't take it with you. If you just buy a bunch of stuff, it's not all going to go in one room and work together. Have a plan, then go for it.

Q What is one item worth splurging on?

A Furniture is worth splurging on because if you buy good, classic furniture, it will last a long time. You can always change pillows and drapes when you want or add new throw pillows. With drapes you can be very trendy and up-to-the-moment. But when you choose furniture, purchase pieces with nice clean, smooth lines that will last and not be trendy.

Q What has been your favorite decorating freebie find, and what did you learn from it?

A I found a wonderful banister that I used as a headboard. I made a table out of a shuffleboard. When you walk by on trash day, there is a treasure trove in people's trash. Most people are just too cool to ask. Well, I ask.

closet in a headboard

Older homes often lack closets, especially in the bedroom. If you have a medium-size or large bedroom, annex significant storage by pulling the bed into the center of the room and partitioning off a closet behind the bed. Prefabricated stud walls create the division between closet and bedroom, so even a novice carpenter can pull off this project like a professional. If your bedroom is large, center the closet wall from side to side in the room; that way the closet can be entered from either side of the bed. Position the storage components back-to-back to create sides for two people.

what you need

Materials

Two 4×8-foot prefabricated
  stud wall sections
  (available through
  special order at home
  improvement stores)
Crown molding, 18 feet
Base molding, 18 feet
Long screws
Finishing nails
Wood filler
Drywall, five 4×8-foot sheets
Drywall screws
Drywall tape
Drywall joint compound
Sandpaper
Paint, in desired colors
Two sets of ready-to-
  assemble modular closet
  storage systems to fit the
  width of the space
  between the headboard
  wall and the bedroom wall
  (the unit shown expands
  from 41½ inches to
  56 inches wide)
Lamp
Wall hooks
Full-length mirror
Wall-hung shoe racks
Laundry hamper

Tools

Measuring tape
Carpenter's level
Cordless screwdriver
Hammer
Nail set
Paint roller
Wide putty knife for
  applying joint compound

1. Set two prefabricated stud wall sections upright and side by side between the floor and ceiling to form one 8-foot-wide headboard wall. (Position the sections so the distance between the headboard wall and the wall behind it equals the width of the storage system.)

2. Stabilize the headboard wall and fasten to ceiling joists and subfloor with long screws. (Use a carpenter's level to make sure the wall is plumb and level.) Fasten drywall to the prefabricated stud wall, front and back, using drywall screws. Finish-nail crown molding to the top of the wall and base molding to the bottom of the wall. Set nails and fill holes with wood filler.

3. Finish the wall by covering drywall seams with drywall tape and smoothing with joint compound. Sand smooth. Reapply compound, let dry, and sand as necessary. Paint as desired. Let dry.

4. Assemble the modular closet units, following the manufacturer's instructions. In the space behind the headboard wall, place the units back-to-back—one side for you and one side for your closet mate.

5. Hang a full-length mirror, shoe racks, and wall hooks (for hats, ties, scarves, and purses). Include a lamp for adequate lighting.

Fabric architecture
Though it's made of fabric, the frame around the window hints at temple architecture.

Gold glimmer
Warm yellow brings a golden glow to the formerly plain white walls.

Exotic art
Overscale artwork features Buddha and Chinese lettering to set the Oriental tone for the room.

Easy seat
A bench provides a spot to sit and put on shoes, filling an empty space on the wall; it serves quietly without encumbering traffic flow.

Stylish feet
The custom-made footboard features feet with a stylish curl—a tiny detail that makes the room even more special.

Look here

Centering the bed along the wall sets the stage for the focal-point headboard: a pair of imported bulletin boards mounted against a brown fabric backdrop.

Heads up

Details do make a difference. A reproduction bust adds mystique to the room.

Sidekicks

Custom-made cube-shape wooden side tables hang on the wall on each side of the bed. They look more expensive than they really are, thanks to rich walnut brown paint.

buddha boudoir

DESIGNED BY EDWARD

Edward transports this master bedroom to a place of serenity and beauty. Styled to reflect one of the homeowner's love of Buddha, the room overflows with fast architectural add-ons and affordable ideas for shaping an import look.

▶Florida: Night Owl Lane

With the bed angled into one corner and white walls all around, this bedroom seems fairly sterile. Only the screen behind the bed hints at some decorative beginnings. The white walls have to go; however, the homeowners voice a dislike for dark surroundings. Can Edward make the bedroom feel welcoming and cozy and still keep the look light? Absolutely!

When the owners of this bedroom ask Edward to create a place where they can "relax and feel like they are in their own little sanctuary," he responds with soothing Asian influences.

"I already have an inspiration and an idea," he says. "I know she is really into the Buddha." Edward develops a design based around the image and starts by making the space inviting with warm yellow wall paint. At the tops of all the walls, elegant black cording is hot-glued in place to stand in as an affordable and fast alternative to moldings.

▶ Secondhand furniture, such as this dresser, can be a dramatic addition to any room if it's given a good painted finish. (Always sand and prime your finds before painting.) To dress up this thrift store dresser and mirrors, Edward opts for brown paint accented with touches of black and gold. To the left of the dresser, curtains conceal the door to the bathroom. The curtains are actually white sheets that Edward decorated with stencils and brown paint.

◀ Edward found two Indonesian bulletin boards and hung them behind the bed as a headboard. Cheap chic!

Edward pulls the bed to the middle of one wall, where it can claim its rightful position as the focal point. A swath of brown fabric behind the bed acts as a backdrop for a pair of Indonesian bulletin boards; these hang side by side to form an exotic headboard. Amy Wynn fashions a footboard with curving feet that she playfully refers to as "a little genie action."

The bed now aligns with the bathroom door on the opposite wall, so Edward conceals the doorway with curtain panels. Brown-painted stenciling adds interest across the bottom of the panels, which are actually white bedsheets retrofitted with a rod pocket.

money crunch $

▶ headboards

Because sleeping is the main activity in a bedroom, it makes sense to put the decorating spotlight on the bed. Adding a noteworthy headboard is one way to prepare the bed for center stage. Consider these cost-efficient options for stylin' the head of the bed:

▶ **SOFT TOUCH.** Cut squares, rectangles, or other shapes from plywood and wrap the pieces with a layer of batting topped with fabric. Staple the fabric edges to the backs of the boards. Use heavy-duty hook-and-loop fastening tape to hang your upholstered creations behind the bed.

▶ **MAT FINISH.** Purchase fabric-edged grass beach mats from an import store. Staple the mats—vertically or horizontally—behind the bed.

▶ **BRUSH UP.** Use painter's tape to outline a block (or blocks) of color behind the bed. Paint the blocks in hues you love.

▶ **MOLDED IMAGE.** Install moldings behind the bed to establish a sense of structure, such as re-creating the look of a fireplace surround; or use moldings to mimic recessed panels.

◄ This horizontal wall-hung shelf does the same job as an armoire for a lot less money. Its clean lines blend well with the placid look of the space.

The homeowners need furniture too, and Edward hits the jackpot at a thrift store, toting back a large dresser, two mirrors, and even a small coffee table—all for an amazing $69. Style comes later when Edward paints the pieces brown and adds black and gold accents. He transforms the coffee table into a bench by putting a cushion on top.

Amy Wynn builds wood cubes to serve as wall-hung night tables on each side of the bed. A third piece—think of it as an elongated cube—hangs on an adjacent wall and holds a small television, books, and a few decorative items. Painting all these custom-made pieces brown ties them visually to the thrift store finds.

wise buys ▼

sheets

Flip through any bedding catalog and you'll see a barrage of phrases, terms, and numbers describing fibers, thread counts, and finishes. Here's what it all means:

▸ **THREAD COUNT.** Thread count refers to the number of threads woven into one square inch of fabric. The higher the thread count, the softer and smoother the bed linens feel. When selecting pure cotton sheets, look for a minimum thread count of 200. When selecting cotton/polyester blends, look for a minimum thread count of 220.

▸ **PIMA AND EGYPTIAN COTTONS.** Pima cotton and Egyptian cotton are different names for the same product. Both terms refer to a specific variety of cotton called ELS (extralong staples) that has more luster and silkiness than standard cotton. Although less common than standard cotton, ELS cotton is grown in the United States and several other countries around the world.

▸ **MUSLIN AND PERCALE.** Sheets with a thread count of 140 to 180 are muslin; sheets with higher thread counts are percale. The finest percale sheets have thread counts of over 300.

▸ **COTTON/POLYESTER BLENDS.** These sheets resist wrinkling, wear well, and are affordably priced. They feel somewhat stiffer than pure cotton percales.

▸ **LINEN.** Linen is cloth made from the fibers of the flax plant. It is the strongest and most expensive of the natural fibers. Linen feels cool against the skin because it conducts heat well; it is ideal for use in hot climates. Its biggest downfall is that it wrinkles easily. When treated to improve crease resistance, linen feels less comfortable against the skin.

▸ **SATEEN, FLANNEL, JERSEY KNIT, AND OXFORD.** These four terms refer to cotton finishes. Sateen refers to a special combed-cotton finish that makes any cotton sheet feel silkier and cooler to the touch. In contrast, nappy flannel finishes provide extra warmth. Jersey-knit cotton sheets are made from the same breathable, stretchy fabric as cotton T-shirts. Oxford cloth, similar to the dress shirting fabric, translates into a soft, heavy sheet. You may find long-lasting oxford sheets in your grandma's linen closet.

▸ **SILK.** Silk sheets are ideal for cold climates because the material traps warmth. The sheets feel smooth and luxurious; however, they are expensive and typically require dry cleaning. Avoid polyester satin sheets, which feel scratchy against the skin.

At the windows, walnut brown fabric makes an arch around each window, forming an outline reminiscent of temple architecture. "It is basically a piece that goes around the window from floor to ceiling leaving a space for the window," Edward says. "[The treatments] make a really big statement, but they use only three yards of fabric apiece."

Between the windows, Edward puts the focus on the empty wall by creating an overscale painting that features Buddha and Chinese characters that mean "luck" and "love"—two emotions anyone is sure to feel in a room as great-looking as this one.

◀ If you can't afford artwork, buy a pre-stretched canvas and paint your own. Edward painted this Buddha and Chinese lettering on canvas, repeating the palette of deep blue, warm yellow, and walnut brown. If painting freehand fills you with dread, use an opaque projector to cast an image on canvas. Outline the image with pencil; then fill in with paint. Below Edward's painting, the thrift store coffee table becomes a chic bench with the addition of a cushion.

From the Designers

▶ EDWARD WALKER

Q If you don't have much of a travel budget, what can you do to explore exotic, international styles—without leaving town?

A Visit your local library and check out books on areas you are interested in. For example, for a Tuscan room, check out books on Italy and neoclassic style. Check out books on Greece or Morocco too. I use the library quite often to get a feeling of a place.

Visit import stores. They seem to be everywhere now! They have pieces from other countries, and you don't have to travel anywhere—except downtown.

Q Where else besides fabric stores can you get amazing deals on cloth and material?

A I always check the thrift stores, consignment shops—even yard sales. Draperies or panels don't have to be used as curtains. You could re-cover a chair or dining room seating with fabric borrowed from a curtain.

Check to see if there is a discount fabric warehouse in your area. There may be one that deals in upholstery fabrics or with a mill in your area.

Even your local superstore can offer good material—and not just in the fabric department. Use towels and afghan throws to make pillows or to cover a chair.

◀ To keep costs for window treatments under control, choose a tailored look that requires only minimal fabric. This fabric treatment by Edward adds the look of a shapely architectural element using only a few yards of low-cost fabric.

thrifty project
inspired by the show

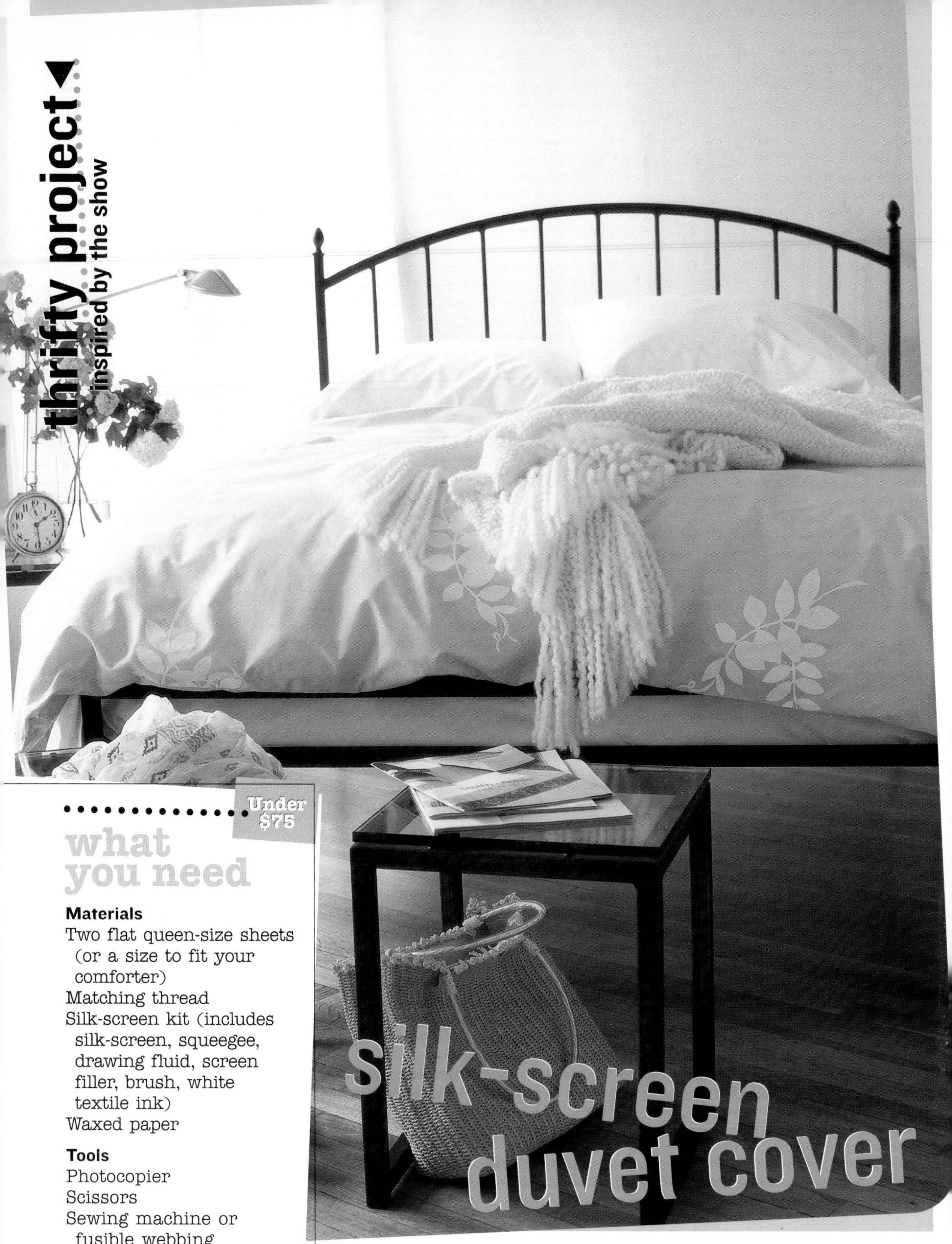

silk-screen duvet cover

Under $75

what you need

Materials

Two flat queen-size sheets (or a size to fit your comforter)
Matching thread
Silk-screen kit (includes silk-screen, squeegee, drawing fluid, screen filler, brush, white textile ink)
Waxed paper

Tools

Photocopier
Scissors
Sewing machine or fusible webbing
Iron
Old toothbrush

Save money and spend some time and creativity making a designer duvet cover out of plain sheets. This European-style duvet cover slips on like a pillowcase over a down- or synthetic-filled comforter. The washable duvet cover keeps the comforter clean and fresh inside and also offers a fast option for changing the style and accent colors in your bedroom.

1. **To prepare the screen for printing,** detach it from the base. Using a photocopier, enlarge the branch design shown here until the branch fills an 8½×11-inch sheet of paper. Lay the screen over the image, topside up, and trace the design onto the screen with a soft-lead pencil. With a small artist's brush, fill in the branch and leaf shapes with the drawing fluid provided in the kit. While you do this, keep the screen elevated; it must not touch the table. Let dry in a level position.

2. **Mix the screen filler.** Spoon the filler onto the screen on the same side as the drawing fluid. Use the squeegee to spread the filler evenly over the screen. Make only one pass if possible—too much filler could compromise the image. Let the screen dry in a level position. Then, using the spray nozzle on your kitchen sink or a spray bottle and *cold* water, spray both sides of the screen and gently brush away the drawing fluid with a toothbrush. Let dry in a level position with the bottom side up.

3. **Wash, dry, and iron** one of the sheets to prepare it for printing. Trim the sides and bottom so that the sheet measures 88 inches square (including the top finished with a wide hem) to fit a full/queen-size comforter.

4. **To print the design on the sheet,** lay the sheet on a flat surface and choose the spot where you want to print the first image. Position a piece of waxed paper under the sheet beneath that spot and then lay the screen over the surface with the flat side facing down. Put a spoonful of white textile ink on the screen. Holding the screen in place, squeegee ink up and down the screen until the image is filled. Carefully lift the screen, holding the fabric in place. Repeat in rows across the sheet. Dry in a hanging position.

5. **Set the prints** (when dry) with a hot iron on the cotton setting; place a cloth between the iron and fabric to prevent scorching. Wash the screen immediately after use.

6. **To make the duvet cover,** lay the printed top facedown on the second sheet. Trim any excess material from the second sheet. Using 1-inch seam allowances, sew the sides and bottoms of the sheets together to make a large envelope of fabric. Leave the top edges unstitched. Turn the duvet cover right side out and stitch on ribbon ties at the open end for closures.

Spicy ingredients
Savory spices yield some tasty color choices, including turmeric for the walls.

Pared down
These once-cluttered open shelves offer a good amount of storage. They look much better with fewer items, neatly arranged.

Corner secret
A bass standing in the corner makes the kitchen more efficient. Turn the page to learn the secret.

DESIGNED BY KIA

Booth beauty
If you have the space for it, extra seating is always a good idea in the kitchen. This salvaged restaurant booth is fun and comfortable.

kitchen harmony

Underfoot cover-up
A neutral-tone rag rug adds softness on the floor and helps conceal some unattractive spots, offering a budget-savvy alternative to new flooring.

If ever a kitchen was out of tune with its homeowners, this one was it. The musical couple could hardly wait for Kia to clear out the clutter and cook up some style. Here's how she plays up their passion for music while making the kitchen more functional.

Encore!

Sheet music, which is applied with decoupage medium and topped with clear nontoxic sealer, hints at the homeowners' love of music.

Geography lesson

If you have space for one in your kitchen, islands have a lot to offer. An island—even a small one such as this—will provide you with storage, counter space, and a place to gather.

▶before

▶ Philadelphia: Cresheim Road

The cook in this house says she has to walk into the next room to get the dishes she needs. That's because the kitchen desperately lacks storage space as well as work surfaces. Cluttered and disorganized shelves make kitchen chores even more difficult. The green walls, plain wood table, and ordinary central light fixture lack style and personality.

▲ If your budget is tight, start decorating with one or two upper cabinets as Kia did here. Patterned glass offers texture and contemporary beauty for a small investment.

◀ Old instruments, especially damaged ones, can often be purchased at bargain prices. This cabinet started with pieces salvaged from an old bass. Amy Wynn fashioned the door to accommodate the found pieces and added a cabinet with a shelf behind the new instrument face.

Both homeowners love music, and one of them loves to cook. However, this kitchen hit some sour notes, offering little in the way of work surfaces, storage, or style. Kia orchestrates harmony by bringing in a new color scheme; she improves kitchen efficiency with some new storage pieces. After the clutter is cleared out, the kitchen walls are brightened with sunny yellow paint that Kia likens to turmeric. White paint makes the trim stand out, and paprika red paint on the base of the new island adds a dash of accent color to the room. Sheet music, decoupaged in place, provides a clever finish for the countertop. Another cabinet—shaped like a bass— plays along with the theme. The brass pot rack is an old trombone. Kia also gives the couple a new countertop and a copper-tone metal backsplash behind the range.

10 Must-Haves for the kitchen

1. **Functional work space.** Make as much as you can out of the counter space you have. If you have room, add counter space with a peninsula, island, or rolling cart.

2. **Storage!** If you don't have room for more, get more out of what you have. Install organizational tools and additional shelves inside existing cabinets.

3. **Attractive and hardworking surfaces.** Splurge on a new floor or an upgraded countertop—they give a kitchen a fresh new look and make cleanup easier.

4. **Excellent lighting.** Combine general and task lighting for good looks and reduced eyestrain.

5. **A friendly color scheme.** The kitchen is the No. 1 gathering area in a home, so choose an attractive, welcoming color scheme to enhance its sociability.

6. **Gathering space.** Because everyone always ends up in the kitchen when you have a party, you might as well offer each person a place to sit or provide an island to stand around.

7. **Eating area.** If you have enough floor space, a snack bar or a breakfast bar can double as a gathering space and make quick meals more comfortable and convenient.

8. **Glass-front or open-shelf displays.** While family and friends are waiting for the food, give them something nice to look at. This also helps cooks find the tools and dishes they need quickly.

9. **Attractive accessories.** Top the counters with an attractive accessory such as a flower arrangement or a set of colorful vases. Make a hardworking space feel less utilitarian.

10. **Electrical outlets.** No one ever complains about having too many.

From the Designers

► KIA STEAVE DICKERSON

Q Can you recommend a good low-cost lighting solution?

A I would recommend considering a ceiling fan with a light. You can customize a basic fan and make it a fantastic focal point. The one I created with the palms on it [for Indianapolis: Halleck Way] was slowed down a bit by the fabric and palm fronds that I attached to the blades. But it fit the Egyptian theme of the room perfectly.

Q How can homeowners effectively introduce color into a room when they don't have enough money to replace the flooring or major pieces of furniture?

A If you're redoing a room that you already have furniture in and you can't afford new furniture or new carpet, pick the focal point in the room that commands your attention and work from there. For instance, if you can't change the mauve carpet, don't pick mauve paint! Pick something more complementary in color as opposed to trying to match it.

▲ Still have your old horn from high school band? Consider bringing it out of the closet and into the kitchen. This trombone pot rack hangs from chains secured to the ceiling with eye screws. (Screw into ceiling joists for stability or use appropriately sized anchor-fasteners.) Brass S hooks hold a collection of pots and pans.

make over your kitchen

before

When you think of a kitchen makeover, you may envision thousands of dollars flying out the window. Inspired by the show, this striking kitchen transformation proves that style can be had for less—sometimes much less—than a grand.

$100

▶ **PAINT, PAINT, PAINT.** Cover blah brown wood and make the kitchen livelier with a multitone paint treatment: Lightly sand cabinets, wipe with a tack cloth, and apply primer; let dry. Paint cabinet bodies white. Paint all recessed door panels and all drawer fronts with rose-color paint; let dry. Paint trim around lower doors aqua. Give upper and lower recessed panels a weathered look by applying white paint over crackle medium; this will allow the rose color to peek through.

▶ **FABRIC FINESSE.** Add cafe curtains. They cover the bottom of the window, reinforcing the cabinet color scheme and adding softness and visual interest.

▶ $100 budget breakdown

paint for cabinets (2 gallons and 1 quart)	$54
hardware	$25
fabric for curtains and valance	$15
rods (2)	$10
blue enamelware teapot	$28
TOTAL	$132

$500

▶STORE MORE. Bring architectural interest and more storage to the kitchen by adding a cabinet over the window. Install this cabinet slightly higher than flanking cabinetry for variety and to allow window operation. Remove the back panel from the cabinet to let sunlight shine through. Replace the recessed wood panels on the doors with grooved glass panels; these diffuse light and allow glassware colors to show. Top the cabinets with crown molding for more character.

▶GLORIOUS COLOR. Set off cabinetry with walls painted bold red—a color plucked from the berries on the curtain fabric.

▶RECYCLE (1). Don't give away the valance. Instead cut the fabric into 5-inch squares (scallop the edges, if you wish); then glue the squares to the wall, evenly spaced, right above the countertop. Protect the fabric with glass panels adhered to the wall with clear silicone. Applied along the top and bottom edges, the silicone resists water leakage.

▶HANGING OUT (2). Add a handy ledge in front of the windowsill for display. Suspend a glass panel level with the sill using steel cables (available at home centers) secured to the bottom of the cabinet above the sink. Have the glass dealer cut the panel to size and drill the holes for the cable. Metal crimps on the looped cable ends support the glass panel from below.

▶$500 budget breakdown

cabinet over sink	$58
crown molding	$15
glass for cabinet door	$40
hanging glass shelf with cable	$25
interior glass shelves (2)	$33
interior light	$19
paint	$28
glass for backsplash	$29
glass bottles (5)	$75
TOTAL	**$322**
PREVIOUS TOTAL	**$132**
NEW TOTAL	**$454**

$1,000

▶**ISLAND ADVENTURE (1).** Customize an antique table to create a convenient rolling island. Add a shelf at the bottom for more storage and to make the table more stable and sturdy. Paint the table base red to match the walls; add casters to the legs so the island can roll where you need it. To make the island work even harder, install a spice rack on the side and racks for wineglasses beneath the tabletop.

▶**BIN THERE (2).** Remove two lower cabinet doors and slip metal bins onto the shelves for decorative punch. These containers allow easy access to potatoes and onions.

▶**FIRST RUNNER-UP (3).** Quickly dress up an ordinary sisal runner with painted stripes.

▶**DYNAMIC DETAILS.** Give the backsplash more dimension and color by hanging a row of round plates along the wall. Find some eye-pleasing accessories, such as an enamelware bowl, to round out your kitchen makeover.

▶**$1,000 budget breakdown**	
kitchen table	$120
lumber to add shelf and support to kitchen table	$25
paint (1 quart)	$10
tool bar and spice rack for kitchen table	$42
casters for kitchen table	$15
knob for drawer	$1
wineglass racks (2)	$15
fabric table square	$15
metal tubs (for storage in open lower cabinet)	$100
rug runner	$48
decorative plates for backsplash	$18
white enamelware bowl	$55
TOTAL	$464
PREVIOUS TOTAL	$454
ROOM TOTAL	$918

High drama

The ceiling makes a power-packed statement dressed with a glowing layer of copper metallic leaf. To provide a rich yet subtle undertone, the ceiling was base-coated in red before the leaf was applied.

Sunny walls

Golden walls complement an array of browns sprinkled throughout the space. The warm hue wraps the room like a cozy blanket.

Floating elegance

A candlelight fixture combines floating candles (in the center bowl) and votives. The metallic-finish ceiling reflects the glow whenever this light is in use.

Radiant review

A trio of candles adds elegance to the bar top for little expense. When the candles are lit, the mirror multiplies the flickering flames.

Bountiful bar

A custom-built bar flanked by manufactured cabinets provides a place to mix drinks and make cappuccinos. Canyon red color and metallic-leaf panels make the bar an enticing place to gather.

Mosaic magic

Italian glass mosaic tiles in earthen hues completely transform the existing pine coffee table, making it a seductive centerpiece.

welcoming outlook

Vern blows the dust off a living room that the homeowners call "a museum." Tired traditional-style clichés give way to a welcoming palette of earthy hues and a fresh furnishings approach designed for entertaining and relaxing.

Sink-in sofa
Ultracushy oversize pillows replace fixed back cushions on this thrift store sofa. Deep brown fabric provides a luxuriant cover-up for the piece.

before

▶ **Pennsylvania: Termont Drive**

**Although traditional style can be lovely,
sometimes the look is unintentionally stiff.
The homeowners recognize that their room
lacks life; they also mention that the room is
dark and that the few lamps they own aren't
adequate in the evening.**

▲ Tall manufactured cabinets store
media components behind closed doors.
They flank a low custom-made cabinet
that offers a preparation counter for
beverages. Combining purchased and
homebuilt storage pieces makes good
economic sense when you want to fill a
wall without spending a fortune. Canyon
red paint unites the disparate pieces,
and metallic leaf on door panels provides
a visual link to the ceiling treatment.

▶ Vern stretched this pricey red and gold linen fabric into four pillows by using plain fabric backing that matches the sofas.

The museum is permanently closed—at least that's what the owners of this living room were hoping when they asked Vern to throw open the windows of style and let some fresh design into the stuffy space. One owner lamented, "It's like a museum. You might as well just put a rope across the door because people walk in the door, look toward this room, and they're not interested in going in."

The couple would love to have a place where they can sit and visit with friends and serve martinis or cappuccinos before or after dinner. They ask Vern to create a space that's loaded with comfort, a room that will lure in friends and family.

"We are going to create a dynamic environment for adults," Vern says. In a surprising move, he starts with the ceiling rather than the walls, painting on a base coat of rich red and topping it with copper metallic leaf—a material that brings a rich glow to the room.

White trim and a golden hue on the walls make the space feel even sunnier. Paint plays another important role in the room by unifying the entertainment center/bar, which is composed of two tall purchased cabinets flanking a long base cabinet constructed by Amy Wynn. For these pieces, Vern chooses an earthy red-brown and glamorizes the doors with metallic leaf.

▲ Creating your own artwork can be exciting if you're rushing to meet a deadline. Vern rendered these appealing beverage-themed pieces, painting them in a pinch—out of money and almost out of time. He mounted the artwork in frames that he borrowed from the neighbor.

money crunch

▶ pillows for a pittance

Watch a few *Trading Spaces* episodes and one decorating truth will become clear: Pillows are one of the most flexible and valuable decorating tools around. For a small investment, you gain color, texture, style, and comfort, all in one neat, easily transportable package. You have a couple of options for expanding your collection of stylish, affordable pillows:

▶ **MAKE YOUR OWN.** Putting together your own pillows is easy, and it certainly saves money, especially if you re-cover pillows that you already have on hand or use loose acrylic fill to stuff pillow covers. (Purchased pillow forms can be expensive.) Cut two pieces of fabric to the desired size and shape, adding about ½ inch all the way around for a seam allowance. Place the right sides of the two pieces together and stitch around three edges (or use iron-on hem tape). Turn the cover right side out and stuff with fill. Stitch the fourth edge closed (or seal with iron-on hem tape).

▶ **EMBELLISH PURCHASED PILLOWS.** Dress up plain pillows with a variety of embellishments, including buttons, fringe, beads, cord, fabric medallions, and appliqués. Secure decorative pieces with stitches, iron-on fusible webbing, a hot-glue gun, or fabric glue.

▲There's no fast way to copper-leaf a ceiling: Work with a helper and apply the individual leaves over sizing. Silver and gold leaf are also available.

▲Positioning a mirror above the central media cabinet makes the room appear larger by creating the illusion that there is space beyond.

▲Glass tiles, such as these used on the coffee table top, offer a look that's richer than traditional ceramic mosaic tiles.

When you're planning a room for parties, you need enough landing spots for drinks. The existing coffee table was recruited for this purpose and given a makeover—not with paint but with Italian glass mosaic tiles—1,244 tiles to be exact. Striving for "calculated randomness," Vern says, he divides the tiles into four batches—each batch comprised of an equal number of caramel, brown, bronze, and copper-color tiles. By also dividing the tabletop into four quadrants, one batch of tiles can be used to fill one quadrant so the tile colors are dispersed evenly but randomly.

Providing enough comfortable seating was another challenge in this room. Vern keeps one existing sofa and adds a thrift store sofa that he purchased for $50. (He was especially happy that the piece came presteamed and precleaned.)

Vern decoratively redeems the existing sofa by snipping off the attached back cushions and replacing them with loose 24-inch-square cushions. Using stuffing from the old cushions to fill the new cushions helped stretch the budget. Walnut brown fabric finishes the sofa update with a rich, contemporary look.

For the thrift store sofa, Vern selects a tan slipcover. Red and gold linen pillows add dashes of color and pattern to both sofas. A daybed/bench/chaise custom-built by Amy Wynn provides additional seating for party-goers and can double as a place to lie down and read or take naps.

A candle chandelier and more candles all around provide a fitting finish for this room with the new, warm attitude. Yes, the museum is definitely closed.

wise buys ▼

upholstered goods

Save hundreds of dollars by buying upholstered furnishings at flea markets and thrift stores. Whether you choose to buy new, vintage, or antique furniture, quality construction and materials are essential concerns for making a good buy.

Most quality manufacturers have a cutaway of the frame and cushions for you to view. If you are unable to see this construction (such as when you are shopping at thrift stores), avoid furniture that shows buckling between parts—cushions and frame, fitted pillow and arm, or wooden and upholstered parts. Squeeze padded areas—you shouldn't be able to feel the frame. A sofa should never sag in the middle— sagging indicates a lack of proper bracing. A sagging sofa will likely sag more (or even break) over time. Gently lean on the piece in different directions to see whether it is sturdy. Tip the piece over to look for maker and material labels. If the muslin covering is loose, peek in at the construction.

▸ **THE FRAME.** No matter how pretty the piece, unless the frame is solid and well-made, the furniture won't wear well. Kiln-dried hardwoods such as birch, maple, and ash are signs of a quality frame. Lightweight softwoods such as pine, poplar, and fir are not as sturdy. Particleboard is strong but more prone to splitting and chipping. Wood joints should be mortise-and-tenon (where one slot-shape piece of wood slides into another) or dovetail (where wood fingers lock together like gears) and secured with glue. These joints are much stronger than butted and screwed joints or glued joints.

▸ **SEATS AND CUSHIONS.** The highest-quality upholstery cushions have inner springs similar to a mattress. The springs are generally covered with a plain fabric then wrapped with polyester batting, a layer of polyurethane foam, and a muslin cover. A decorative upholstery cover zips over all of this. Medium-quality cushions are made from a solid piece of polyurethane foam covered in polyester batting. A muslin cover is sewn over the cushion, then the decorative upholstery cover is zipped in place. When made from high-quality materials, these cushions can last for years. Lower on the quality scale are cushions made from a single piece of polyurethane foam with a decorative cover sewn permanently in place. Although not long lasting or overly comfortable, this construction has its place, such as for short-term use in a child's room, college dorm room, guest room, or first apartment.

▸ **UPHOLSTERY FABRIC.** The fabric of an upholstered piece is the most visible sign of quality and also the part most likely to show wear or age. Fabric cost and grade do not necessarily reflect quality. A lower-cost and lower-grade canvas is likely to be more durable than a more expensive, higher-grade, lightweight damask. Heavy fabrics such as canvas, tapestry, woven wool, and leather are generally more durable than lightweight fabrics such as satin, taffeta, chintz, and linen. Plush and napped fabrics may crush with wear. Textured weaves and subtle patterns help hide dirt and soil.

Under $125

what you need

Materials

Ready-to-assemble console table (this one measures 48×16×30 inches)
Fine-grit sandpaper
Tack cloth
Acrylic paints: white, aqua pearl, blue pearl
Containers for mixing paint
Brown paper bag
Clean, lint-free rags for painting
Disposable plastic gloves (optional)
6 to 8 pounds of flat-sided decorative marbles (also called mosaic marbles) in various sizes and blues, greens, and pearl colors
Industrial-strength adhesive or epoxy
Paper
¼ yard each of three different fabrics (to make the fish)
Matching threads
Polyester fiberfill
22-gauge wire

Tools

Paint roller
Carpenter's level
Long straightedge
Pencil

'something's fishy' console table

Why clean an aquarium when you can enjoy the maintenance-free undersea adventure of this console table? Paint, fabric fish (that you'll never finding floating on the surface), and loads of glistening glass "bubbles" create a watery depth that pleases the eye.

1. Assemble the table according to the manufacturer's directions. Sand all the surfaces and wipe them clean with a tack cloth. Paint the table with two or three coats of white acrylic paint, allowing the paint to dry between coats. Use a brown paper bag to lightly sand the dry painted surface between applications to smooth any raised grain.

2. Pour small amounts of aqua pearl and blue pearl paint into separate containers. Add a small amount of water to the paint and stir to bring each color to the consistency of cream. Place a rag over your fingers and dip it into the aqua pearl paint. Using a swirling motion, rub the paint onto the tabletop, including the edges. Allow the paint to be uneven and let some of the white show through; this will give the finish a watery look. Immediately apply a layer of blue pearl in the same manner, letting some of the aqua pearl and a

small amount of white show through. Finish with a light layer of aqua pearl to add depth. Let paint dry.

3. Arrange the marbles around the outside edges of the top. Be sure to leave enough space in the middle so the top is usable. When you're pleased with the arrangement, glue the marbles in place. Tip: Use a small amount of glue for each marble and wipe away excess glue.

4. After the glue dries, lay the table so that the back side is down; glue marbles to the front apron and legs, decreasing the amount of marbles as you work toward the bottom of the legs. Let glue dry. Turn the table upright.

5. Draw three fish onto paper and cut them out. The ones shown range in size from 4×6 inches to 6×9 inches. Cut two pieces of each fabric slightly larger than the fish pattern to allow for seam allowances. With the wrong sides of the fabrics facing, pin the patterns to the fabric. Cut three 4-foot-long pieces of wire. Sandwich the center portion of each wire between the fabric layers of a fish, placing it through the center of the fish body. Sew around the fish just

outside the edge of the pattern; sew over the wire. For flat fish, sew completely around the fish. For puffy fish, leave an opening for stuffing. Work a small amount of fiberfill into the fish. Sew the opening closed. Remove the pattern and trim the fabric close to the stitching.

6. Loop the wire into a loose circle and hold it under the table to determine the length of the hanging loop. Twist the wire to close the loop; trim away the ends. Use a staple gun to secure the loops to the underside of the tabletop. Arrange the wires and fish as desired.

DESIGNED BY RICK

safari chic

Think of the romance and adventure of Africa in the early 1900s, and you'll appreciate even more the billowy tent, tribal art, and river rock red walls in this family room. The tent provides a sense of shelter and comfort—and a place to stash toys.

Divine divide
The first layer of mystery consists of matchstick blinds set in a dark brown-red frame. The blinds filter and stylishly frame the view of the adjoining kitchen.

Luxurious gathers
The front of the shelter culminates in a valance replete with luxurious gathers, which are held in place by straps of matching fabric. Leather laces thread through grommets in the ends of the straps and are tied around a rod suspended from the ceiling.

Romantic refuge

Forming a room within a room, this tentlike structure achieves a seemingly impossible juxtaposition of airy and cozy moods. The ivory cotton fabric makes the outward appearance light and breezy; the lush folds and generous billows make the interior cozy and sheltering.

Golden sky

Rich golden-yellow paint on the ceiling radiates like the sun overhead.

Stamped style

You may look at potatoes with more respect when you learn that this delicate design was stamped onto the fabric with carved spuds dipped in wall color.

Warm walls

Dressed in paint the color of a river stone, the walls exude natural warmth.

Worth reusing

Existing leather furniture, such as this inviting chair, got this room off to a handsome start.

Elegant anchor

A classic rug, such as this red and ivory specimen, could take a good chunk of the budget, but it's worth the investment when you know it will never go out of style.

▶ **Ohio: Shelby Avenue**

The owners of this family room would like Rick to devise a way to store the toys out of sight. White walls don't do much to set off the black coffee table and leather furnishings, which are all nice pieces. Because the space is open to the kitchen, Rick must consider how to cope with the connection as he shapes the design.

▼ The owners had nice leather furniture to inspire their new scheme. If leather is too rich for your budget, check out catalogs and online resources for affordable slipcovers. Suede and faux-suede slipcovers are readily available for many chair and sofa sizes and styles.

◀ To make the divider, the neighbors glued the matchstick panels to a painted 1× frame. Matchstick blinds are exceptionally inexpensive and come in a variety of sizes. Look for some of the best prices at home centers and online. Trim the blinds to length by cutting between the matchsticks with scissors. Carefully tie off the ends of each string to keep the remaining matchsticks in place.

money crunch $

▶ textured wall treatments

Paint purchased with sand already in the mix gives this room a slightly primitive dimension. Consider these low-cost ways to bring texture to walls:

▶ **SANDY ALTERNATIVE.** Add your own sand to a gallon of paint. Purchase a bag of clean sand and add only ¼ cup of sand at a time until you achieve the desired texture.

▶ **EUROPEAN VINTAGE.** Lend a charming, old-world feel to walls by mixing four handfuls of 2- to 6-inch-long strands of straw into 1 gallon of drywall compound. Use a 6-inch putty knife to apply a thin coat of the mixture to primed walls. If needed, use your fingers to move pieces of straw into more-attractive patterns. Let dry. Apply a layer of thinned paint or glaze in the desired color.

▶ **SHADOWS OF NATURE.** Start with a selection of herbs, leaves, shells, and rocks with interesting surfaces. Apply a thin coat of textured paint over a primed wall. Dip the collected items in water and randomly press them into the still-wet compound. Pull the objects away, leaving their imprints behind. Let dry. Then protect and highlight the wall with pigmented glaze.

▶ **MORE CREATIVE COMPOUNDS.** Use a trowel or a 6-inch putty knife to apply drywall compound to the wall. Experiment with designs (first try this on a scrap piece of drywall), sweeping the compound into swirls, fan shapes, or wavy lines. Have fun!

A long with the joys of parenthood come truckloads of toys and playtime paraphernalia. Of course, Mom and Dad supervise the baby's play, so all those things show up where everyone hangs out most often. In this case, the gathering space is a family room belonging to the parents of an 18-month-old boy.

"I pick up on clues," Rick says, "and the first clue I'm picking up here is that the late-20th-century toy store look needs to go away. The other clue is that [the homeowners] seem to do this jungle/African theme, then they ran out of steam."

The homeowners' existing leather furnishings and primitive art accessories serve as a foundation for a look from the plains of Africa and the romance of "roughing it in style," complete with a billowy tent of ivory cotton fabric. The tent, which fills a wide niche at one end of the room, creates an elegant sheltered sitting area within the family room, and the back fabric panels hide shelves for storing toys and media equipment.

Separating the sectional sofa into individual seating creates a more lively arrangement. A triangular occasional table between two seats provides a place for displaying animal and ethnic figures.

pillows

Whether you're in the market for new bed pillows or making a few toss pillows for the sofa, choose the right filling for the job:

▸ **DOWN.** Made up of tiny goose and duck feathers, down is soft, plush, and more expensive than other fillings. It requires frequent fluffing to maintain its shape and is not typically considered suitable for allergy sufferers. However, specially cleaned down (and feather mixtures) works well for some people with allergies. Pure white goose down is considered the best quality.

▸ **DOWN AND FEATHER MIXTURE.** More affordably priced than pure down, this mixture is firmer and less plush. Allergy sufferers should purchase pillows filled with specially cleaned down and feathers.

▸ **FEATHER.** Goose feathers are the best quality; duck feathers come in second. Feather fillings are more resilient than down and moderately priced. Allergy sufferers will want specially cleaned feather varieties.

▸ **SYNTHETIC FIBER.** This is a good choice for people who are allergic to down. Affordably priced, polyester puffs mimic the performance of down but are more resilient.

▸ **FOAM RUBBER.** This inexpensive material is considered hypoallergenic and can be sculpted for specific sleep-style support. It is much firmer than the other fillings, but it loses its resiliency over time, so it will need to be replaced more often. It is often used in combination with other synthetics to create pillows designed for specific purposes such as shoulder, back, and neck support. Consult with a doctor before investing in these specialty pillows.

NEED NEW BED PILLOWS?

Place the pillow on the floor and fold it in half. For down or feather pillows, squeeze the air out. When you release it, the pillow should unfold and return to normal shape. For synthetic pillows, place a medium-size tennis shoe on the folded pillow. The pillow should spill the shoe, unfold, and return to normal shape. If your pillows don't return to normal shape, it's time to invest in some new ones.

▶ Rick assembled this collection of exotic art and figurines (available at import stores for reasonable prices), pairing the pieces with a bamboo lamp on a custom-made table. A matchstick-panel inset outlined with rope ties the table visually to the room divider.

Though the existing furniture provided a good starting point, the original white walls were lackluster. Rick sets off the breezy fabric with walls painted earthy red. Mixing sand into the paint introduces subtle texture to the walls—a tactile bonus that suits the rustic elegance of the room.

Complementing the tent are window treatments fashioned from the same airy ivory cotton fabric. Cotton fabric straps, painted the wall color, pull the curtain panels up into folds reminiscent of the billowed sides and top of the tent.

Between the family room and adjoining kitchen, a new divider made of matchstick blinds on a 1×4 frame provides definition without closing off the connection between rooms.

brushes and rollers

You've probably noticed by now that nearly every room makeover begins with fresh paint. Purchasing quality brushes and rollers that will last for years makes good economic sense. Quality painting tools also ensure even application and clean up better and faster than low-cost look-alikes.

▷ Quality brushes are thick with springy bristles that don't shed. On the best brushes, the bristles have split ends known as flags. These allow the brush to retain more paint and spread it more uniformly. Inexpensive brushes have silky bristles that tend to break easily.

▷ To paint large surfaces such as ceilings, walls, and floors, use a flat wall brush that is 4 to 6 inches wide and 1 inch thick.

▷ To paint medium-size areas such as cabinets, tabletops, and picket fences, use a flat dash brush that is 2 to 3 inches wide.

▷ For woodwork and other trim, use an angled trim brush that is 1 to 2 inches wide.

▷ Quality rollers feature a solid core that feels firm and a nap of thick, durable fibers that doesn't shed when rubbed. These rollers hold paint better than less-expensive versions, reducing drips and spatters. Low-cost rollers typically have a hollow core that may bend and flatten over the course of the job; the nap may shed and stick to wet paint.

▷ The roller handle you choose also makes a difference. Ergonomically designed handles provide more comfort as you grip the roller. Roller extension poles allow you to reach higher on the wall without the aid of a ladder.

In addition to brushes and rollers, you need to keep a few more tools on hand for most painting jobs: drop cloths, ladders (see page 83 for more information), buckets with liners (to reduce cleanup), roller pans with liners (again to reduce cleanup), a paint edger (for trimming ceiling lines, doors, windows, and baseboards), painter's tape, and clean, lint-free rags.

◀ Muslin and white cotton duck are two low-cost options for making window treatments. Watch the bargain bins at fabric stores for even better deals. For these window treatments, additional strips of fabric accented with wall paint were used to gather the curtain panels.

iron-on
fiesta

what you need

Materials
2 queen-size flat sheets in the desired solid color
Matching thread
Paint or colored markers
Iron-on transfer paper designed for ink-jet printers

Tools
Iron-on transfer software kit for ink-jet printers
Ink-jet printer and computer
Scissors
Sewing machine
Pencil
Iron

Transform a plain pair of queen-size flat sheets into a fun, fiesta-inspired tablecloth. You'll create the iron-on designs yourself, using an ink-jet printer, a computer, and iron-on transfer software.

A.

B.

1. **To make a round tablecloth** from two queen-size flat sheets, fold one sheet in half twice and mark the desired radius along the wide open edge. Cut a string the same length as the radius you just marked. Hold one end of the string at the closed point of the folded sheet; hold the other end of the string in your other hand along with a pencil. Use the string to guide the pencil mark in the desired arc. Cut along the arc and unfold the sheet. Repeat the steps with the second flat sheet; it will serve as a liner for the tablecloth. Stack the circles of cloth with right sides together and stitch around the outside edge, leaving a ½-inch seam allowance. Leave a small portion unstitched for turning. Turn the tablecloth right side out and hand-stitch the opening closed. Press.

2. **Dream up a design for your tablecloth** (and plan matching napkins, if you wish). Use paint or colored markers to draw your designs. Or take photographs and scan them into your computer to use later. For this tablecloth, guacamole and its ingredients are the theme—perfect for a party. Simple paintings of yellow lemons and green avocados provide color. Scan your designs on a flatbed scanner and save on your computer. Or have a copy center scan your art and provide you with data files.

3. **Type words or phrases** that you want to appear as a border for the tablecloth, using a word-processing program. For this tablecloth, the words are the ingredients for guacamole. Select a font and lettering size that you like.

4. **Following the instructions** on the iron-on transfer software kit, print the lettering in mirror-reverse onto the iron-on transfer paper. Make a few test runs on plain paper so

you can later position the transfer paper with the correct side up in the printer paper tray.

5. **Print the colored designs** on iron-on transfer paper as well, in mirror-reverse, if you wish (see Photo A).

6. **Cut out the individual letters** so that you can align the words or phrases to follow the curve of the tablecloth. Also cut out the designs. Position the lettering and designs as desired. Follow the instructions with the iron-on transfer kit to transfer the lettering to the fabric. Generally, you lay a pillowcase on a hard surface, such as a laminate countertop. Lay the tablecloth on the pillowcase with the letters or designs in position. Use a hot iron with no steam. Iron each letter for the recommended time, using heavy pressure on the iron (see Photo B). Let transfers cool, as recommended in the instructions, and gently peel off the paper backing.

Zippy zinnias
Like a dream, gigantic freehand zinnias float around the room, introducing a joyfully blooming palette of pretty pinks and yellow centers.

Glad plaid
Pink and green plaid, wrapped around layers of batting and stapled to a plywood board, becomes a merry headboard when set into a frame built by Amy Wynn. For continuity the headboard mimics the style of the mirror frame above one dresser.

Throw a party
Customize a blanket to create a comforter that fits the room theme: Cut the fringe, if any, from a purchased throw. Stitch on a backing of a second fabric and use a third complementary fabric to edge the throw.

DESIGNED BY LAURIE

zinnias for kids

Goodbye clutter
Corral all the stuff in stylish containers. Amy Wynn built these boxes, and Laurie personalized the fronts with monograms. Turn to page 121 for more toy storage ideas.

Fruity foundation
A contrasting backdrop makes the posies pop out from the walls. Laurie calls this fruity hue pear green.

Girlish details
Pear green curtain panels feature a petite pattern of flowers. Candlewick stitching on the lampshade is feminine and fun.

Pucker up
A formerly white storage piece now sports a zesty lemon yellow look.

Real chenille
Search online and at flea markets, and you can still find chenille bedspreads for bargain prices—in a variety of hues and motifs. The nubby texture is inviting and soft. Cut damaged spreads to make pillows or throws.

The happy memories of childhood often include special spaces, especially ones that featured fanciful designs and magical colors. Laurie delightedly dresses this suite, which is shared by two sisters, using a garden of cheerful hues, playful plaids, and giant painted zinnias.

▶before

▶Pennsylvania: Bryant Court

**This spacious bedroom includes a pair of twin
beds, one painted dresser, and one wood
dresser. The light-color walls are pretty, but
not pretty enough to keep two young sisters
enchanted. The parents tell Laurie that they
often find their daughters curled up in sleeping
bags on the floor of the master bedroom.**

T his kid suite didn't have the drawing power that the
parents had hoped for. Rather than staying tucked in
their own beds, the little girls preferred sleeping in
sleeping bags on the master bedroom floor. It's little wonder then
that the homeowners asked Laurie to give their daughters a room
that little girls dream about.

Colors that look like they came from a bowl of fresh tropical
fruit make the room fanciful and fun. After painting pear green on
the walls, Laurie pencils huge zinnias all the way around the
room, spacing them randomly and even allowing a few petals to
float up onto the ceiling.

Once the flowers are drawn, the petals are painted white and

▶Kids love to put their artwork on
display, so a bulletin board is a welcome
addition to the bedroom. Laurie made
this bargain board out of thin cork squares
that are attached to the plywood backing
with adhesive.

he centers yellow. Pink petal shapes form the next painted layer,
aving crisp white outlines that make the flowers so dimensional
hey practically leap off the walls.

Lemon yellow and white serve as the perfect paint partners,
iving the existing furniture new panache and playfulness.
helves supported by charming flower-shape brackets hang
eside one dresser and are painted to match.

Though paint plays a major role in the room, it's the beds that
ecome the stars. Laurie made ordinary twin-size mattresses
eem fit for a pair of princesses when she designed tall
eadboards with plumb center panels that are upholstered in
ink and green plaid. Amy Wynn made the headboard frames

► Toy boxes can be basic. Though these are custom-made, plain wood storage crates with a fresh coat of paint would function equally well.

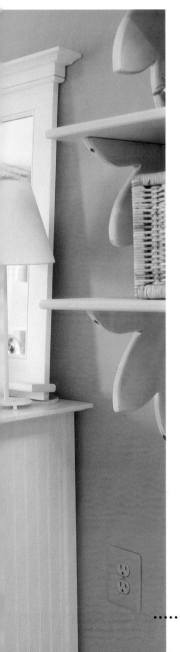

money crunch

► toy storage

Try these other easy and inexpensive ideas for stowing and storing kids' playthings:

► **WICKER CONTAINERS.** Baskets made of wicker come in all shapes and sizes, and many styles feature lids. Hunt for bargain baskets at crafts stores and import stores.

► **WIRE BASKETS.** These work well for rounding up stuffed animals and larger toys.

► **CLEAR PLASTIC STORAGE BINS.** If kids can easily see what goes where, they'll be more likely to put things away. Clear plastic storage bins let the colors of the toys show through for fun and function.

► **UNFINISHED TOY CHESTS.** If you want to try your hand at painting, decoupage, or some other fun finish, check crafts stores and home centers for unfinished toy chests. You can also start with a stained or painted piece and customize it to suit your child's personality.

even more special by adding moldings across the top to mimic the style of a dresser mirror.

Soft-as-a-cloud chenille bedspreads, pear green and plaid throws, and pillows to match and contrast ensure that the beds will beckon to the little girls.

Laurie provides some features to make the room easier to pick up too, including custom-built toy boxes—monogrammed with each little girl's initials—and some baskets and shelves. A bulletin board fashioned from cork squares glued to a piece of plywood provides a spot to display artwork and photos of friends, family, and pets.

"Zany for zinnias," Laurie says with a delighted smile at the end of the episode. "I love their random quality and how they fold up across the ceiling."

▲ A basic white lampshade turns beautiful when you add beaded borders. Stick beads on with hot glue formulated not to melt under the heat of a lightbulb.

From the Designers

▶ LAURIE HICKSON SMITH

Q If you had only $100 to pump up the style of a space, how would you spend your money?

A Fabric. New throw pillows, a slipcover for a sofa—just something to add some spice. On a limited budget, I would rather see something tactile added to the room, then move on to paint. For example, if I had any money left over after adding new throw pillows to a neutral sofa, I'd pull the paint color from the pillows.

Q You get to see homes all over the United States. What's the most common problem with home decorating today?

A I think there has been a mindset over the last 10 years that bigger is better. I don't know which came first—the buildings or the furniture. Oversized, overstuffed furniture is what the mainstream sells, and it's unfortunate. I walk into these homes, and the furniture is so overscale that it's not proportionate to the space. So we try to accommodate big furniture by having sprawling homes with open interiors and tall ceilings. But you end up losing intimacy and character.

Q Where do you go for decorating inspiration?

A If I can't find a fabric or passion to inspire me, I will often pull down an art book from the shelf and start flipping through. I'm so inspired by how artists put color palettes together. Deep, rich eggplant with pecan green, for example. I might even be inspired by how an artist made a color combination on a tea caddy.

10 Must-Haves for any bedroom

1. **Beautiful bed.** An attractive headboard or canopy can make this nightly necessity a decorative focal point.

2. **Attractive storage.** You need a place to stash your underwear, socks, and in many instances, TV.

3. **Personalized color scheme.** The palette needs to feel welcoming to everyone who shares the space.

4. **Lovely linens.** Select linens that feel as good as they look.

5. **Light-controlling window treatments.** Not everyone wants to get up with the chickens.

6. **Cherished displays.** Who doesn't want to wake up looking at their most treasured memorabilia?

7. **Bedside table.** You have to set the cookies and milk somewhere.

8. **Reading light.** Whether you're the reader or the snorer beside him or her, you'll want a task light that complements both activities.

9. **Full-length mirror.** You can be certain your shoes match your shirt if you include one of these on the back of a closet door.

10. **Alarm clock.** Hey, you have to get up and get started on your room makeover!

◄ New shelves give the girls a place to store stuff. Baskets such as these are inexpensive and sized to store crayons, markers, cards, and other small objects.

lights
fantastic

A.

what you need

PAPER LANTERNS

Materials
Purchased paper lanterns
and light kits
Tissue paper or crepe
paper in desired colors
Matte-finish decoupage
medium

Tools
Large decorative paper
punch and/or scissors
Foam brushes

If you're sitting around in a room that's too dark, let there be light! These two projects will help you brighten the room while adding dashes of color and great style. Make more than one of either project and hang in groupings wherever you need to dispel shadows.

Paper Lanterns with Pizzazz

1. **Unfold paper lantern** according to package directions.

2. **Cut or punch out** desired shapes from the tissue or crepe paper.

3. **Brush decoupage medium** onto the paper lantern where you want to add decorations. Lightly tap the tissue paper onto the decoupage medium, checking that all of the edges stick. If the dye of the paper doesn't run when brushed with decoupage medium (check before you place the tissue on the lantern), brush a light coat over the top of the paper (see Photo A).

4. **Cover the entire surface** of the lantern with designs and decoupage medium. Let dry.

5. **Hang the lantern** using a light kit designed for your type of paper lantern. Follow the manufacturer's directions and safety instructions.

Tip: To stabilize the lantern while decorating it, set the rounded lantern in a wide-mouthed bowl. This keeps the lantern from rolling around as you apply decoupage medium and also frees your hands to do the delicate work of attaching the tissue paper.

Hanging Candle Fixture

1. **Use pliers** to open individual links and separate the chain into three equal lengths. The length of the chains will determine how low the fixture hangs.

2. **Spray-paint** the metal bowl inside and out. Also spray-paint both sides of the wicker coaster to match. Lightly spray-paint the three lengths of chain and the cup hook to reduce the shine of the metal. Let dry.

3. **Attach the coaster** to the underside of the basket with glue, centering the coaster on the base of the basket.

4. **Attach the chain lengths** to the rim of the basket by opening the last link with pliers just enough to slip the link onto the basket rim. Space the chain lengths equally around the rim.

5. **Screw the cup hook** into the ceiling. Slip the other end of the chain lengths over the cup hook to suspend the basket from the ceiling.

6. **Place the candle** inside the basket.

get the look ▲

Illuminating idea
Lights installed in the tops of the columns help illuminate the room and add another unexpected element.

Around the block
Rectangles in three shades of gray stack up for high style in this high-ceilinged bedroom.

Fresh start
Though these are the existing bed linens, the subtle tones and simple stripe pattern suit the new color scheme.

Screen stars
The traditional four-poster bed didn't fit the contemporary theme. Wire screen mesh columns—crumpled for sculptural appeal—stand in as silvery replacements for the wood posts.

Ceiling savvy
Dark brown on the ceiling makes this oversize bedroom feel more intimate and warm.

Storage style
Individual cabinets, which Ty dubbed "solitary confinement cells," line up along one wall to meet a variety of storage needs.

Bar none
Using the existing window blinds keeps the project on-budget, and the simple styling is perfect for the streamlined look of the room. Metal conduit "bars" are just for fun.

DESIGNED BY DOUG

prison of love

Though Doug's "Prison of Love" bedroom theme could be ruled as tongue-in-cheek, no pardons are necessary. The resulting multiple shades of gray, the graphic-block wall pattern, and a dramatic twist on a traditional four-poster bed assure that you'll judge this design fabulous and unforgettable.

No one will ever accuse designer Doug Wilson of keeping his creative courage under lock and key. Setting his more mischievous side free, Doug has some extra fun with this oversize bedroom, dubbing it the "Prison of Love."

An empty expanse above a plant shelf high on the wall of the vaulted bedroom sparks the idea. "For some reason, in my twisted mind," Doug says, "I saw bars and a mural up there. Because so often spaces like these get neglected and become a dust collector for fake plants. So I really wanted to do something interesting."

To fill in the blank space, Doug envisions a wall mural depicting the second tier of a prison—complete with real bars fashioned from metal conduit.

Starting with three shades of gray for the walls and deep brown for the ceiling, the neighbors paint rectangular blocks on

►before

►Columbus: Shelby

Plenty of space and dramatic high ceilings give this master bedroom a terrific start design-wise. The homeowners say they have 16 good years from their traditional cherry-wood dressers and four-poster bed—all a wedding gift—but they are ready for a change. They're hoping for color to dress up the all-white walls and a place to stow the television set.

◀Doug bought these porcelain bench bases—actually commodes—for only $37 each. While his idea could be tongue-in-cheek, salvage yards are an excellent source of low-cost pieces and materials that you can adapt or re-purpose for other uses. Above the bench, candle sconces are fashioned from mesh wire screen folded accordion-style and stapled to half-round wood pieces, which hold the candles.

the walls, extending the pattern from floor to ceiling, and outlining each shape with painter's tape to assure crisp edges. They leave the space above the plant shelf blank so Doug can paint the mural.

Though the neighbors playfully liken the painted pattern to cement blocks, the resulting design is elegant and graphic. But the new contemporary look initiated by the walls definitely doesn't suit the existing traditional cherry-wood bedroom set. It's no wonder then that Doug and Ty launch the episode wielding chainsaws, which they rev up and use to quickly lop off the tall posts on the four-poster bed.

Doug dreams up a method for modernizing the bed: Silvery wire screen mesh is rolled and softly crinkled into sculptural floor-to-ceiling columns and installed as four gleaming posts for the bed. Lights introduced inside the tops of the posts produce a pleasing glow for evenings. Candlelight sconces fashioned from additional mesh wire screen offer mood lighting around the room.

◀New homes often feature high ceilings and tall walls, leaving empty expanses that do little to enhance the space. A painted mural is an affordable way to introduce color and interest.

money crunch

▶ affordable painted surfaces

Whether you're dealing with large expanses of walls or a worn wood floor—or even one recently installed—painted designs can give these blank slates fresh character. Keep these basics in mind:

▸ **Make sure that walls are clean and free of grease and grime. Fill holes with spackling compound, let dry, and sand smooth before painting.**

▸ **If the floor is previously finished or painted, lightly sand the finish and thoroughly vacuum up the sanding dust.**

▸ **For walls or a floor, select high-quality paint for the job. Some paints are specially formulated for floors, but to ensure long wear you can protect high-quality paint with an acrylic sealer.**

▸ **Apply the base coat of primer, using a roller with a long handle to save your knees and back. Let dry thoroughly—at least overnight for floors. Humid conditions may demand additional drying time.**

▸ **Roll on the base coat and let dry thoroughly.**

▸ **For floors or walls mark a design using a pencil and appropriate tools, such as a straightedge, a carpenter's level, or a carpenter's square. When making especially long lines, snap a chalk line. You can tape off the straight edges of designs to achieve crisp lines. Or use stencils or stamps to create a design. Be careful not to paint yourself into a corner! Let designs dry thoroughly.**

▸ **Protect your work on floors with at least three coats of clear, nonyellowing, water-base poly-acrylic. Let each coat dry thoroughly before applying a subsequent coat.**

With all these special pieces coming into play, no ordinary armoire would do. Instead, Doug devises a row of freestanding storage closets with small window cutouts fitted with metal conduit bars. Ty cheerfully builds the pieces and calls them solitary confinement cells. Painting the pieces dark gray assures that the cabinets look great in the room while offering an abundance of storage.

Doug finishes the room with fun flourishes: Two commodes stand in as a porcelain base for a wood bench top, metal conduit slips in as easily removable "bars" at the windows, and the prison mural takes shape above the plant shelf.

"Besides the mural," Doug says, "the bedposts are my favorite thing in the room. There is nothing in this room that can't be quickly altered."

◀ The painted blocks give this room its graphic appeal for only the cost of paint. Wire mesh for the sconces (as well as the bedposts) can be purchased in bulk rolls to control costs.

◀ Deep gray paint ties the new cabinets to the painted blocks on the bedroom walls. Building cabinets such as these from MDF keeps them affordable. If metal bars aren't your style, consider filling cutouts with textured or colored glass and include lighting inside the cabinets to produce a soft glow as well as adequate illumination to view what's inside.

▲ Wire screen mesh is easy to manipulate into columns such as these or to fold accordion-style to create wall sconces. When working with wire of any kind, always wear thick gloves to protect your hands from cuts.

wood
and wood-look floors

Improvements in technology and manufacturing make both **solid wood** and wood-look **laminate** floors easier to care for and less costly to install. Either material is a good choice for a flooring makeover. Both of these flooring types are available in glueless tongue-and-groove designs that snap together, eliminating the need for nailing and gluing. These floating floors also can be unsnapped and removed, making it possible for renters to enjoy the beauty of a wood or wood-look floor without having to leave it behind when they move.

In addition to unfinished planks and parquet tiles that have to be stained on-site, **natural hardwoods** are now available with pre-finished urethane surfaces that provide higher scratch- and abrasion-resistance for extended wear. Although seemingly more expensive than their unstained counterparts, the reduction in installation costs makes them a comparable buy. Like all wood, these pre-finished floors are vulnerable to prolonged moisture.

While **laminate** has been used on countertops since the 1940s, it has only been readily available as a flooring material since the 1990s. Slightly less expensive than real wood, the most recent introductions look even more realistic and are more durable than the laminates commonly used on countertops. Although extremely durable, the flooring can be scratched by heavy furnishings and cannot be repaired; however, individual planks can be replaced. Even glued-down installations have a slightly hollow feel when compared to real wood. Some of the best varieties feature a waterproof synthetic core that eliminates the potential for water damage caused by seepage beneath the surface. When combined with tight-fitting laminate edge moldings, these new surfaces can be used in moisture-heavy bathrooms and kitchens.

easy artwork on canvas

If your walls are bare and your bank account is looking a little spare as well, purchase pre-stretched artist's canvases at crafts stores and make your own art. Start with only one or two canvases and build your collection as your budget allows. If you determine a color palette and stick with it, your artwork can hang in a cohesive grouping as shown here. Even if you have little or no experience painting, the following three techniques will make you look like a pro.

·········· **Under $15 per canvas**

what you need

Materials
Canvas
Acrylic crafts paints
Low-tack painter's tape or masking tape
Plastic plate or container for mixing paint colors
Water

Tools
Paintbrushes
Drinking straws
Hair dryer

Crisp Designs

Go graphic and edgy with the help of masking tape or low-tack painter's tape.

To leave a white strip of canvas, tape a design onto the blank canvas and paint over the tape. Cover the entire canvas with paint as desired. Before the paint dries, gently peel off the tape to reveal the white lines.

To create colored strips, paint the entire surface of the canvas in the desired color. Let dry thoroughly. Tape a design over the painted canvas and paint up to or across the tape as desired. Before the second color dries, gently peel off the tape to reveal the first coat of color. Layer additional taped designs as desired.

Streams of Color

Get a trippy, hippie effect with thinned paint and a little breeze.

1. **Mix crafts paints** with a small amount of water until mixture has the consistency of milk.

2. **Stick a drinking straw** in the paint mixture, cover the top of the straw with your finger to create suction, and hold the straw over the canvas. Remove your finger, dropping the paint on the canvas.

3. **Using a hair dryer** or blowing through the straw, blow the paint into streams of colors running in various directions across the canvas. Continue the process, layering different colors on top of one another.

Blended Beauty

Create subtly shifting bands of color with this easy technique.

1. **On a blank canvas,** brush thick strips of two different colors close to each other.

2. **Slowly pull a paintbrush** through the two colors of paint, pulling the two colors closer to each other. As the colors start to touch, continue pulling the paintbrush through the colors, eventually merging the edges of the colors.

3. **Brush over the blended portion** several more times. You can choose to lightly work the colors into each other so there is a third strip of color that consists of streaks of the two original colors. Or you can blend them to the point where the third strip of colors is a true mix of the two original colors.

Tip: Create as many strips of color as you like, using any number of colors.

get the look ▼

In the spotlight
Track lights are inexpensive and install easily. This one features adjustable spotlights that focus on the artwork.

Monochromatic curtains
Curtains match the wall color to keep the look uninterrupted.

Gallery chic
Soft, sensuous colors swirl across a trio of canvases that hang side by side in a gallery formation known as a triptych. Hildi painted these with an ordinary trim brush.

Calm color
Paint colors are allowed to merge and flow on this canvas, creating an ethereal image that enhances the tranquil mood of the room.

Sofa soother
Because the sofa isn't the highlight here, Hildi selected one with simple lines. The slipcover blends with the surroundings, allowing the sofa to remain unobtrusive without sacrificing comfort.

calm and cool

DESIGNED BY HILDI

Hildi clears the clutter out of a living room and wraps the walls, window, and sofa in soothing shades of soft blue. Worn carpet gives way to a gorgeous brick floor. With nothing to distract, artwork and an artistic coffee table become simple pleasures.

▶before

▶**Miami: Ten Court**

White walls and rattan furniture with flame-stitch fabric-covered cushions make this room dated and unexciting. An overabundance of toys creates clutter. "The room could use a focal point," says one of the homeowners.

▶ Wood l× slats and spacers are the main ingredients of this benchlike coffee table. Even if woodworking isn't one of your strong suits, you can join wood slats side by side using finishing nails and wood spacers. Adapt the idea by setting the tabletop on a base of glass blocks. Put a light inside the blocks for a pleasant evening glow.

The homeowners admit that their living room lacks a focal point, and the husband isn't thrilled with the wicker furniture. Hildi envisions something lower-key and more elegant. "This room needs a lot of change," she says. "This room is going to look like a simple gallery, and everything that is here is going to be out of here."

After completely clearing the room of furniture, toys, and even the carpeting, a backdrop of soft blue is added to the walls. Hildi then reveals the highlight of the space: flooring tiles that are made of polymer-modified cement and molded to look like bricks. Laying the tiles requires much of Day I, but Hildi reassures everyone that it's worth the effort. "When we are done with the floor," she says, "everyone's going to want it. Trust me." As the floor grout sets, Hildi re-covers a streamlined sofa she found at a thrift store for $50, using blue fabric to match the walls. Removing the cushions from the back of the sofa keeps the look low and unobtrusive. Finishing the room are several pieces of artwork painted by Hildi and the neighbors. Three tall canvases hang side by side on the wall opposite the sofa. New track lights aimed at the canvases keep the colors on display when the sun goes down.

"It's a totally fresh start," Hildi says with satisfaction. "Now it's a gallery space—very calm, soothing, and a place to just sit back and admire the art."

◀ Small canvases like these, which Hildi placed elsewhere in the room, are affordable and can be found at crafts and art stores. If you're contemplating large-scale art, however, take a cue from Hildi and save money by constructing 2×2 frames and stretching the canvas over the frames. Use a staple gun to secure the edges of the canvas to the back of the frame pieces.

wooden sheet goods

When you plan to build a project that you want to stain, MDF won't do. Instead consider reasonably priced plywood for the job.

For a smooth, attractive outside layer, choose A-rated plywood. The material is very strong because the grain in each layer runs perpendicular to the grain of adjacent layers; the A rating means the outside layer will have only minor blemishes. Birch plywood is popular because its grain is light and the surface looks good painted or stained. Oak or birch plywood is available at home centers and lumberyards. It costs $30 to $35 for a ½-inch-thick 4×8-foot sheet.

Because the edges of plywood aren't attractive, you'll need to decide how to cover them. A number of options are available, including wood veneer strips made to match the veneer on the plywood. You can also cut dimensional lumber to fit along the edges; choose a wood that matches the veneer or select wood that contrasts. Secure the wood strip with wood glue and finishing nails; clamp overnight. Countersink the nailheads and fill the holes with wood filler. Once the filler dries, sand lightly and finish as desired. You can also use other materials to finish edges, such as metal strips for a contemporary look.

make over your living room

Though this living room is furnished with comfortable pieces, the arrangement lacks function and interest. Tired traditional style and wimpy pillows need some pumping up too. Inspired by the show, this makeover begins as the homeowners erase a choppy two-tone paint treatment on the walls and wainscoting. Watch a total living room transformation happen in $100, $500, and $1,000 phases.

before

$100

▶ $100 budget breakdown	
paint (2 gallons)	$50
pillows and fabric	$50
TOTAL	**$100**

▶**COHESIVE BEGINNING.**
Paint wainscoting and walls in one rich golden-brown hue to warm the room and to create a cohesive backdrop for furnishings and accessories.

▶**PILLOW IMPROVEMENTS.**
Make seating more inviting with plumper pillows. Reuse existing pillows by wrapping them in layers of acrylic batting and sewing new covers. Purchase new, larger pillows too. Mix real and imitation silk to keep the budget in check; stick with a collection of solid, chic hues.

▶**INSTANT DRAPERY UPDATE.** Remove tiebacks from curtain panels and let the panels hang straight for a streamlined look.

▶$500 budget breakdown

chest and embellishments	$200
large artwork	$40
lamp	$60
end table	$60
TOTAL	$360
PREVIOUS TOTAL	$100
NEW TOTAL	$460

$500

▶MOVING MOMENT. Rearrange the furniture for a new look and to improve traffic patterns through the space.

▶SIDE DISH. Provide plenty of landing places for beverages, books, and snacks by adding a side table next to the sofa. Clear the coffee table and add a large, low-slung bowl borrowed from another room.

▶TREASURE CHEST (1). Energize the room with a stylish industrial element that provides additional storage and display space: Purchase a flea market chest of drawers and glue galvanized metal panels on the drawer fronts and side panels. Sand the panels with an orbital sander to create a matte finish. New amber glass knobs complement the wicker tones in the room.

▶THINK BIG (2). Create drama behind the sofa with oversize artwork. Start with a large piece of $\frac{1}{8}$-inch-thick hardboard (this one measures $3\frac{1}{2} \times 4$ feet). Brush on a rough, primitive coat of paint in several creamy tones; let dry. Mount a small oil painting (perhaps a garage sale find) on a piece of black cardboard near the top of the rectangle as shown. Hang the new art above the sofa.

▶LIGHT IT UP. Play up the sleek new look by topping the chest with a stainless-steel lamp.

▶MAKE A TRADE. Swap the traditional floor lamp for a simpler version—toted in from another part of the house.

$1,000

▶STYLISH STRIPES (1). Highlight windows with new treatments fashioned from ready-made panels. Customize the panels with horizontal 12-inch-wide brown faux-silk stripes.

▶ACQUIRE AN ACCENT. Select a clean-lined accent lamp for the side table. Add sparkle all around the room with extralarge clear glass vases. Keep the designs sleek so the look is sophisticated and chic.

▶TAILOR-MADE (2). Shape up the existing slipcover and make it appear more custom-fit. Remove the ties, pull the fabric tighter around the sofa, and cut off the excess. Add a neat row of buttons along each side as shown.

▶BOXED BEAUTY. Search catalogs for nifty display features, such as the stair-step grouping of brown boxes on the wall. Top off the boxes with a contrasting collection of white vases.

▶TABLE TRANSFORMATION. Update the existing coffee table with a coat of chocolate brown glaze applied to the painted surface with rags. Protect and enrich the glazed finish with a coat of tinted furniture wax. Trade the glass top for a mirror to reflect candlelight.

▶CHAIR LIFT (3). Latch on to a flea market slipper chair for a retro touch. Make a slipcover from green silk and include an inverted pleat with a covered button on the back. Allow a little leg to show.

▶RIBBON FINISH. Embellish the floor lamp by attaching ribbon to the edges of the shade.

▶$1,000 budget breakdown

chair and slipcover fabric	$150
fabric for window treatment	$50
lamp on end table	$50
boxes and vases	$100
mirror	$50
glass vases	$100
ribbon	$3
buttons	$6
TOTAL	**$509**
PREVIOUS TOTAL	**$460**
NEW TOTAL	**$969**

▶ **budget work**

OK, let's be frank. Budgeting isn't the most exciting of topics. In fact, creating a decorating budget can be downright awful! For this reason, the worksheets and calculators in this section are designed to be some of the easiest, most straightforward budgeting tools you'll ever use. You'll hit the ground running with price-scouting activities and then kick into high gear with easy-to-use templates. Knowing how much a project will cost depends on knowing how much of a particular decorating material you'll need, so we've included calculators to help you accurately predict how much paint, flooring, lighting, and other materials your makeover will require.

shop

become a price sleuth:
ESTIMATING COSTS

Getting a sense of how much your next room makeover is going to cost is absolutely critical to carrying out a redo that is successful in terms of both appearance and budget. The best way to gauge future expenses is to take a few hours and scout prices at several home centers or hardware stores. Consider visiting a few discount or department stores too, where you'll round out the decorating details for your makeover project. To get the most out of this exploratory shopping trip, follow these tips:

▸ Set aside an entire morning, afternoon, or evening to scout stores and gather information. You're not purchasing; you're merely comparing prices. You'll need several hours to comparison shop. However, overplanning may keep you browsing for months. Set a reasonable time limit.

▸ Talk with customer service representatives, especially at home centers. Ask them about products you're interested in. Find out how difficult items are to install, ask if you can learn to install them yourself, and make a list of supplies and tools you need to buy or rent to completely install each item.

▸ Take along a small notepad. Use a separate page for each store or each item you're investigating. When you return home, remove your notes from the pad and organize the various pages to get an overall view of the products and prices for your room makeover.

To get a ballpark sense of how much a redo may cost, review the following table of comparative costs for various decorating and design materials; note the price ranges of items you may need for your next room redo.

Keep in mind that these prices are only averages and are helpful for rough-planning purposes. Prices almost always vary from store to store and from region to region. To cut cost, watch for good sales and always call around for the best deals.

Item	Lower End	Higher End
FLOORING *(per square foot)*		
Vinyl tile or vinyl sheet flooring	$1	$5
Ceramic tile	$2	$12
Laminate	$4	$5
Hardwood	$6	$14
Carpet	$1	$10
Professional installation	$2	$6
WALLS		
Paint (per gallon)	$8	$25
Wallpaper (per roll)	$10	$150
Molding or trim (per linear foot)	$1	$5
LIGHTING		
Table lamp and shade	$20	$200
Floor lamp and shade	$30	$400
Chandelier	$50	$1,500
Hanging pendent fixture	$35	$500
Ceiling fan	$60	$600

Item	Lower End	Higher End
WINDOW TREATMENTS *(for one 32" × 60" window)*		
Roller shades	$10	$60
Plastic blinds	$15	$50
Metal blinds	$20	$70
Wood blinds	$40	$150
Valances	$25	$100
Curtains	$30	$150
CABINETS *(per linear foot)*		
Ready-made cabinets, limited finish and door style selection	$50	$200
Semicustom (fixed sizes with fill-in panels to fit space available), broader choice of finishes and styles	$150	$400
Custom (any size, shape, style, or finish you want)	$250	$1,000
COUNTERTOPS *(per linear square foot)*		
Laminate or ceramic tile	$15	$50
Solid-surfacing	$80	$150
Stainless steel	$10	$20
SINKS		
Enameled steel	$100	$200
Acrylic	$150	$400
Stainless steel	$65	$2,000
Cast iron or solid-surfacing	$200	$1,200
FAUCETS		
Basic chrome with plastic cartridge	$40	$150
Solid brass with metallic finish, ceramic disk valves	$150	$350
Brass, nickel, copper, pewter in various finishes	$200	$300
Contemporary or reproduction designer models	$300	$600
FURNITURE		
Upholstered sofa	$250	$2,500
Upholstered chair	$100	$1,500
Upholstered ottoman	$80	$900
End table	$40	$400
Coffee table	$90	$700
Console table	$75	$600
Entertainment center	$75	$1,000
Dining table for four	$75	$800
Dining chair (wood)	$25	$200
Twin bed frame, headboard, and footboard	$100	$800
Twin bed mattress and box spring	$300	$800
Twin bedding set	$60	$250
Full/Queen bed frame, headboard, and footboard	$150	$1,000
Full/Queen bed mattress and box spring	$500	$1,500
Full/Queen bedding set	$80	$500
King bed frame, headboard, and footboard	$200	$1,200
King bed mattress and box spring	$800	$2,500
King bedding set	$120	$700

breaking down the COSTS

To arrive at an accurate estimate of how much your project will cost, you need to break the job into parts or projects. Make a list of each of the projects you'll complete (for example, paint four walls lime green); also list new components you'll need to purchase for your makeover (for instance, a new ready-to-assemble computer workstation). Then look at each project and each new component and plug in costs based on the research you did during the price-sleuthing phase of your project (see pages 144–145). Here are some suggestions for doing the cost breakdown:

▶ Go into as much detail as possible. However, it's not necessary to calculate minutiae (for example, how many cents you'll need to spend on masking tape for a wall-painting project).

▶ Do what professional contractors and builders do: Estimate a 10 to 15 percent "surprise margin" into your final total budget to help cover unexpected expenses along the way.

▶ Look at the sample budget that follows and then use the blank worksheet on the opposite page for your next makeover project.

▶ BUDGET WORKSHEET TEMPLATE
Cost Estimates for My Caribbean Bedroom Makeover

Description	Quantity	Cost Per Unit	Total Cost (qty. × unit cost)	Source/Store	Purchased? Comments
PROJECTS TO COMPLETE					
Project #1: Painted Walls					
Aqua paint	2 gallons	$19	$38	Hardware store	Yes
Texturized roller	1	$13	$13	Hardware store	Yes
Luminescent glaze	2 quarts	$10	$20	Crafts store	No
Project #2: Gauze Canopy					
Gauze	12 yards	$8	$96	Fabric store	Yes
1-inch bamboo poles (for frame)	4 poles	$5	$20	Home center	No
Twine	1 roll	$2	$2	Crafts store	No. Need to pick up.
Project #3: Lighted Nightstands					
Wicker wastebaskets (2 for each nightstand)	4	$12	$48	Department store	Waiting for next month's sale.
Lamp kit	2	$6	$12	Discount store	Yes
Lightbulbs	2	$1	$2	Discount store	Yes
Project #4: Stenciled Rug					
Sisal floorcloth	1	$80	$80	Home center	Need to research.
Stencil paints	4 tubes	$5	$20	Crafts store	Yes
Tropical stencil	1	$7	$7	Crafts store	Yes
NEW COMPONENTS TO PURCHASE					
Bamboo table lamps	2	$25	$50	Discount store	Yes
Tropical bedding set	1	$89	$89	Department store	No. Waiting for next month's sale.
Potted palm tree	1	$32	$32	Floral shop	Yes
Wicker pot	1	$10	$10	Floral shop	Yes
Wood miniblinds	3	$85	$255	Discount store	Yes
TOTAL PROJECT COST			**$794**		

BUDGET WORKSHEET TEMPLATE
Cost Estimates for My_____Makeover

Description	Quantity	Cost Per Unit	Total Cost (qty. × unit cost)	Source/Store	Purchased? Comments
PROJECTS TO COMPLETE					
Project #1:					
Project #2:					
Project #3:					
Project #4:					
NEW COMPONENTS TO PURCHASE					
TOTAL PROJECT COST		$			

With the following handy-dandy lists, you'll always have the right tools and supplies for any job. The items are separated into two categories: those that you really must have to complete the task and those that are nice to have if you have the budget. Remember that you don't need to purchase every tool that's on the market. Use the following lists to prioritize and plan strategically for your next purchases.

For Fabric Projects

MUST-HAVES:

- ☐ Embroidery needle
- ☐ Iron and ironing board
- ☐ Fabric glue or fusible hem tape
- ☐ Tape measure
- ☐ Sharp cutting shears or crafts knife
- ☐ Straightedge

NICE-TO-HAVES:

- ☐ Permanent marking pen
- ☐ Sewing machine or serger
- ☐ Staple gun and staples
- ☐ Sewing patterns
- ☐ Self-healing cutting mat and rotary cutter

For Paint Projects

MUST-HAVES:

- ☐ Water- or oil-base primer
- ☐ Paint (latex/water-base is easier to clean up and produces fewer fumes)
- ☐ Lint-free cotton rags
- ☐ Blue painter's tape and low-tack adhesive tape
- ☐ Plastic drop cloth
- ☐ Assorted paintbrushes (synthetic bristles for latex paint, bristle fibers for oil); specific brushes include:
    - ☐ 1- to 2-inch angled sash brush for painting trim
- ☐ Rollers
- ☐ Roller pan
- ☐ Stepladder
- ☐ Surface compound for filling small holes
- ☐ Putty knife or drywall knife
- ☐ Fine- and medium-grit sandpaper

NICE-TO-HAVES:

- ☐ Stain-blocking primer, to cover water and smoke stains
- ☐ 4-inch brush for painting broad expanses
- ☐ Steel wool
- ☐ Tack cloths
- ☐ Crafts knife and extra blades
- ☐ Disposable cups and plates
- ☐ Donut-shape corner roller
- ☐ 6-foot ladder
- ☐ Roller bucket
- ☐ Plaster patch or joint compound for big holes
- ☐ Paint comb, to clean brushes

For Lighting Projects

MUST-HAVES:
- [ ] Lamp kit
- [ ] Lightbulbs
- [ ] Voltage/current tester
- [ ] Pliers
- [ ] Wire cutters
- [ ] Screwdriver
- [ ] Lamp base/shade

NICE-TO-HAVES:
- [ ] Fabric shade
- [ ] Decorative finial
- [ ] Specialty lightbulb
- [ ] Extension cord
- [ ] Ribbons, beads, and paint for base and shade embellishment

For Window Treatment Projects

MUST-HAVES:
- [ ] Drill and bits
- [ ] Iron and ironing board
- [ ] Tape measure
- [ ] Level
- [ ] Ladder

NICE-TO-HAVES:
- [ ] Fabric glue or fusible hem tape
- [ ] Sewing machine or serger
- [ ] Specialty curtain hardware

For Canvas Wall Art Projects

MUST-HAVES:
- [ ] Small nails
- [ ] Level
- [ ] Tape measure
- [ ] Pre-stretched canvas
- [ ] Paintbrush
- [ ] Paint, markers, ink
- [ ] Plastic plate for mixing

NICE-TO-HAVES:
- [ ] Canvas
- [ ] Wood framing pieces
- [ ] Picture wire
- [ ] Decorative frame
- [ ] Specialty paint and brushes

For Building Projects

MUST-HAVES:
- [ ] Drill and bits
- [ ] Hammer
- [ ] Tape measure
- [ ] Fine- and medium-grit sandpaper
- [ ] Level
- [ ] Pliers
- [ ] Adjustable wrench
- [ ] Crafts knife and extra blades
- [ ] Crosscut handsaw
- [ ] Hacksaw or coping saw
- [ ] Safety glasses or goggles
- [ ] Gloves
- [ ] Respirator

NICE TO HAVES:
- [ ] Ruler
- [ ] Nail set
- [ ] Plumb bob
- [ ] Carpenter's square
- [ ] Chalk line
- [ ] Caulk gun and caulk
- [ ] Staple gun and staples
- [ ] Circular saw
- [ ] Jigsaw
- [ ] Tablesaw
- [ ] Electronic stud sensor
- [ ] Power sander and sanding disks
- [ ] Router
- [ ] Sawhorses

how much **stuff** do you need?

Ideally you would never come to the final stages of a makeover and realize that you don't have enough of a key material to finish the job. At the same time, overstocking supplies to avoid this situation could leave you with too much extra material and a major budget drain.

Use the calculating tools on the following pages to estimate accurately how much paint and flooring you need to purchase. Also, make the best choice in window treatments, shelving, and lighting with the easy measuring and planning advice.

►HOW MUCH PAINT DO YOU NEED?

Although many paint manufacturers claim that one gallon of paint will cover 400 square feet, you're better off estimating 300 square feet of coverage per gallon. Always buy slightly more paint

than you need. You'll be glad you have the extra for touch-ups and in case you spill any. Also, some surfaces soak up more paint than others. (For example, plaster absorbs more paint than drywall, paneling, or wallboard; unfinished wood absorbs more than finished or treated wood.) Refer to the illustration for details.

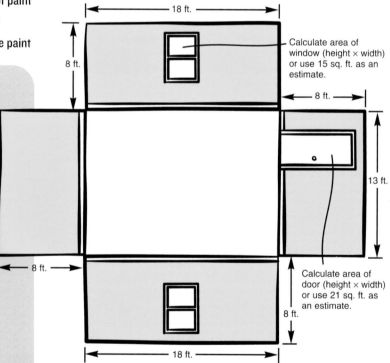

Calculate area of window (height × width) or use 15 sq. ft. as an estimate.

Calculate area of door (height × width) or use 21 sq. ft. as an estimate.

►TO CALCULATE WALL AREA:

1. Add wall lengths to find perimeter.
   13 + 13 + 18 + 18 = 62 ft., in this example.
2. Multiply the perimeter by the wall height. Most homes built in recent decades have a wall height of 8 feet, but measure your room to be sure.
   62 ft. × 8 ft. = 496 sq. ft.
3. Find the area of doors and windows. Estimate 15 sq. ft. of area for each standard window; 21 sq. ft. for each standard door.
   15 sq. ft. × 2 + 21 = 51 sq. ft. of windows and door area.
4. Subtract door and window area from the total square footage.
   496 sq. ft. – 51 sq. ft. = 445 sq. ft.

►TO CALCULATE CEILING AREA:

1. Multiply room length by room width.
   18 ft. × 13 ft. = 234 sq. ft.
2. Subtract area of skylights and light fixtures, if significant.

►TO CALCULATE NUMBER OF GALLONS YOU NEED FOR ONE COAT:

1. Divide the wall area by 300, which is the average coverage in square feet for a gallon of paint.
   445 sq. ft. / 300 = 1.5 gallons of paint
   This number is for one coat of paint.
2. Multiply by the number of coats you plan to paint. Remember that going from light colors to dark—or from dark to light—may require more than two coats of paint.
3. When in doubt, round up.

►HOW MUCH FLOORING DO YOU NEED?

To figure out how much flooring material you need for a rectangular room, multiply the length by the width and then add 10 percent. For example, a 10×15-foot room needs 150 square feet of flooring material, plus 15 additional square feet (10 percent). The extra flooring will ensure that you have enough material for the job. Some stores will take back unused material; however, keep some extra for later repairs.

If your room has counters or protruding closets, subtract the square footage these obstructions occupy from the overall area of the room. Begin by taking the overall dimension of the room by the widest dimension. Then measure the length and width of each obstruction. Subtract the area of each obstruction from the overall square footage, add 10 percent, and then head for the store.

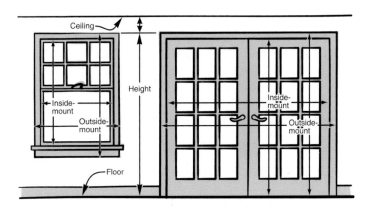

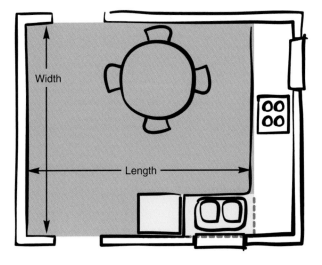

▶ **MEASURING FOR WINDOW TREATMENTS.** You'll purchase the right window treatment the first time, every time, if you take the key measurements shown in the illustrations. Most windows are not square, so always take each measurement in three different

places along the edge you're measuring. Use the smallest of the three measurements when you select the window treatment. Round your measurements to the closest ⅛ inch.

▶**CALCULATING FOR SHELVING.** Shelves and brackets are an easy way to boost the storage potential of any space. Precut shelves in various lengths and materials are available at home centers and discount stores. When planning shelving, consult the following table to calculate the appropriate span, that is, the space between brackets.

The potential for sagging depends on how much load a shelf will bear. A shelf of books requires more supports (short spans) or thicker shelving material than a shelf holding linens. The maximum span depends on if the load is concentrated in the center of the shelf or distributed along its length.

▶ Finding the area of odd walls

▶ **WALLS AROUND STAIRS.** To find the area of walls around stairs, divide the wall into two triangles and a rectangle, as shown in the illustration.

1. Determine the area of the two triangles. Multiply the length of one triangle by its height and divide by 2. Repeat for the other triangle.

2. Determine the area of the rectangle. Multiply the length by the height.

3. Add the three areas together to get the total square footage.

▶ **GABLED WALLS.** To find the area of gabled walls, measure the wall as if it were a rectangle. Multiply the height by the width to find the total area.

Shelf span

Material		Maximum Span with a Heavy Load	Maximum Span with a Light Load
⅜-inch plate glass	6 inches wide	15 inches	24 inches
	12 inches wide	18 inches	36 inches
½-inch acrylic plastic	6 inches wide	18 inches	30 inches
	12 inches wide	20 inches	36 inches
1-inch lumber	6 inches wide	18 inches	36 inches
	12 inches wide	24 inches	48 inches
¾-inch particleboard	6 inches wide	20 inches	36 inches
	12 inches wide	28 inches	48 inches
¾-inch plywood	6 inches wide	24 inches	48 inches
	12 inches wide	36 inches	54 inches
2-inch lumber	6 inches wide	36 inches	48 inches
	12 inches wide	48 inches	60 inches

how much lighting do you need?

Lighting is one of the most underrated design tools around. Decorating the *Trading Spaces* way will help you put each of your rooms in the best light. Start by including the following three types of lighting in all your rooms:

▶**AMBIENT.** Also called general lighting, ambient lighting is the overall illumination in a room. Though one central fixture can sometimes satisfy ambient lighting needs, most rooms are more pleasing when the general lighting comes from a blend of sources. As a guideline, provide at least 100 watts of incandescent light or 25 watts of fluorescent light for each 50 square feet of floor space.

▶**TASK.** This is the light that illuminates a specific activity to prevent eyestrain. Reading, putting on cosmetics, and chopping vegetables are all examples of activities that require a higher level of light that's specifically directed. Provide the task area with 150 watts of incandescent light or 25 to 35 watts of fluorescent light.

▶**SPECIAL-EFFECT.** This is lighting that sets a mood or accents the best features in the room. Track, recessed, or wall-mounted fixtures provide useful accent illumination. Some indirect-light techniques include positioning an uplight behind a plant or using a ceiling- or wall-mounted fixture to cast soft light on a textured wall, artwork, or fireplace.

You can also set a mood and control light with a dimmer. These special yet inexpensive controls allow you to adjust the intensity of illumination that is emitted from a fixture or series of fixtures. For example, control bathroom lighting with a dimmer so you can take a long, relaxing soak in a softly lit, quiet space.

Consider these common types of bulbs for your lighting plan:

▶**INCANDESCENT** bulbs are inexpensive, but they don't last particularly long. Most of the energy they consume produces heat, not light. They're a good choice for lights that are rarely used, such as in a closet.

▶**ENERGYMISER OR SUPERSAVER** bulbs are incandescents that use 5 to 13 percent less energy than traditional incandescents with minimal reduction in light output. They cost more but use less energy. Use these bulbs in moderately used fixtures or for anyone who doesn't like the glare of fluorescent lighting but wants to save energy.

▶**HALOGEN** bulbs are more efficient than incandescents and last three to four times longer. These are great for track lights and spotlights because you can use a lower-wattage bulb yet get the illumination that larger-watt incandescents provide. Some halogen fixtures have the added advantage of being small and can produce a very concentrated white light; this makes them ideal for providing directed accent lighting.

▶**COMPACT FLUORESCENT** bulbs screw into the same sockets as incandescents. They use about 75 percent less energy than incandescent bulbs and last 10 times longer. They cost more yet save many times their purchase price by cutting energy use.

Now that you know the types of lighting and the bulbs that can be used, study the floor plans, *opposite*. These illustrate the four most common types of rooms and some possible lighting plans. Let your needs and the particulars of your space dictate how many lights you incorporate.

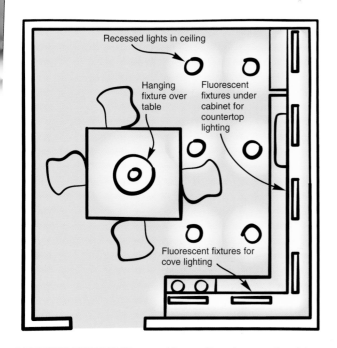

▲ **IN THE KITCHEN,** recessed fixtures offer unobtrusive ambient lighting. For a 9-foot-high ceiling, choose 5-inch-diameter downlights and position them about 12 inches from the cabinets to help illuminate upper-cabinet interiors and countertops. For undercabinet lighting, choose fluorescent tubes that extend over two-thirds of the counter length.

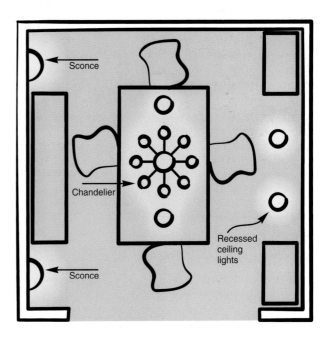

▲ **IN THE DINING ROOM,** if you plan to install a chandelier above the dining table, choose one that matches the scale of the room. As a general rule, select a fixture that measures 12 inches less in diameter than the width of the table. Hang the fixture high enough to allow eye contact between diners. Augment your plan with recessed spots for task lighting and sconces to set a mood.

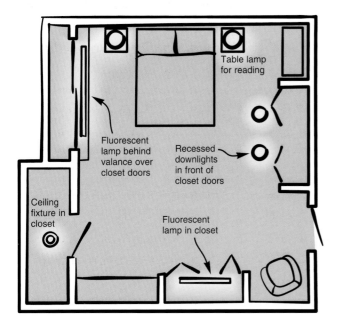

▲ **IN THE BEDROOM,** plan lighting for reading, selecting clothing, and dressing. For reading, flank the bed with lamps or secure spotlights to the headboard. A single incandescent or fluorescent fixture in the center of a closet can provide ample light. Or use a long fluorescent tube as shown in the illustration. If the closet lacks space, install recessed fixtures outside the closet doors but away from the bed to avoid glare.

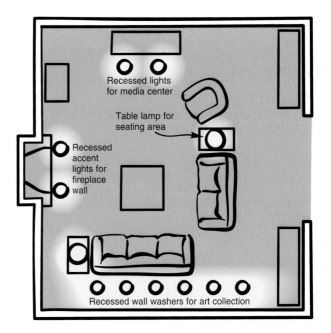

▲ **IN THE LIVING ROOM,** provide good ambient lighting by positioning two table or floor lamps so they align diagonally; or use three lamps to align triangularly. These lamps can also provide ample light for reading. Recessed fixtures can offer additional task lighting, such as in front of a media center to illuminate controls on a DVD player. Mood lighting can include recessed wall washers for art and recessed spotlights for the fireplace wall.

episode guide

Whatever your decorating needs, style, and budget, there's a *Trading Spaces* episode sure to inspire your next project!

You already know that each episode of *Trading Spaces* is absolutely bursting with fantastic decorating inspiration for every budget and style. But how can you possibly keep track of all those hundreds of rooms and projects?

Fret no more, fans! Consider the following sections your personal *Trading Spaces* programming guide.

▶ **THE EPISODE GUIDE** that begins below chronologically lists and describes every *Trading Spaces* episode, Seasons 1 through 3.

▶ **THE DECORATING IDEA INDEX** that begins on page 168 helps you identify episodes in the list that match your specific decorating needs in terms of room type, colors used, major projects, themes, and more.

For more information and helpful before and after photos from each episode, check out *Trading Spaces Ultimate Episode Guide* (©2003, Meredith Books) or visit http://tlc.discovery.com/fansites/tradingspaces/tradingspaces.html.

Who knew watching television could be so inspiring?

Season 1

E1: Knoxville, TN: Fourth & Gill
Cast: Alex, Frank, Laurie, Amy Wynn
In the premiere episode, Frank brightens a den by using a faux-suede finish in shades of gold on the walls, reupholstering the homeowners' Arts and Crafts furniture, and painting two armoires in shades of red, gold, and black. Laurie punches up a bland kitchen by painting the walls electric pear, retiling the floor in large black and white checks, and using chrome accents. She also creates an organized family message and filing center.

E2: Knoxville, TN: Forest Glen
Cast: Alex, Doug, Hildi, Amy Wynn
Doug creates a romantic bedroom, which he titles "Country Urbane," by painting the walls sage green, building an upholstered bed, pickling (whitewashing) an existing vanity, and making a privacy screen. Hildi designs a sleek living room, painting the walls a dark putty color and a thin black stripe around the edge of the wood floor, sewing white slipcovers and curtains, hanging spotlights on the walls to showcase the homeowners' art, and building end tables that spin on lazy Susans.

E3: Athens, GA: County Road
Cast: Alex, Frank, Hildi, Amy Wynn
Frank brightens a child's room by painting the walls lavender, hanging a swing from the ceiling, making a wall-size art area with chalkboard spray paint, and spray-painting a mural of white trees. Hildi updates a kitchen/living room area by painting the dark wood paneling and ceiling ecru, hanging cream draperies, slipcovering chairs with monkey-print fabric, building shelves to showcase the homeowners' pewter collection, enlarging the dining area by ripping out a portion of the carpet and laying vinyl tiles, and painting several pieces of furniture black.

E4: Alpharetta, GA: Providence Oaks
Cast: Alex, Hildi, Roderick, Amy Wynn
Hildi re-creates a dining room using the existing dining table, aubergine paint, horizontal wall stripes of a high-gloss glaze, pistachio-color curtains, two-tone slipcovers, a striking star-shape light fixture, and a privacy screen. Roderick brightens a den/guest room by painting off-white stripes on the existing khaki walls, stenciling a sun motif in a deep rust-red, slipcovering the furniture with an off-white fabric, and installing a wall-length desk that can be hidden with curtains.

E5: Lawrenceville, GA: Pine Lane
Cast: Alex, Dez, Hildi, Amy Wynn
Dez adds a feminine touch to a dark wood-paneled living room by whitewashing the walls, painting the fireplace, and dismantling a banister. She finds new ways to display the husband's taxidermy and decoy duck

collection, which includes a custom duck lamp. Hildi brings the outdoors in, creating an organically hip living room with a tree limb valance, wicker furniture, minty-white walls, and an armoire covered with dried leaves.

E6: Buckhead, GA: Canter Road
Cast: Alex, Genevieve, Laurie, Amy Wynn
Gen gets wild in a kitchen by painting the walls electric pear, adding silver accents, using colanders as light covers, painting the existing formica counter top brown, and removing cabinet doors. Laurie creates a crisp living room by painting the walls chocolate brown, laying a sea-grass rug, hanging a white frame on a large mirror, and adding cream and white slipcovers and curtains.

E7: Washington, D.C.: Cleveland Park
Cast: Alex, Dez, Doug, Ty
Dez creates a funky-festive living room by combining electric pear, white, gray, black, and red paint in solids, stripes, polka dots, and textured faux finishes. She adds unusual lighting to the room by building a three-headed Medusa lamp complete with spiky lightbulbs and Christmas lights. Doug goes retro in a basement by making a beanbag sofa and a kidney-shape coffee table with legs made of plastic tumblers. He also paints the walls bright orange stenciled with white geometric shapes.

E8: Alexandria, VA: Riefton Court
Cast: Alex, Frank, Genevieve, Ty
Frank cozies a country kitchen by creating a picket-fence shelving unit and using seven pastel paint colors to create a hand-painted quilt on the walls. Gen goes graphic in a living room, enlarging and recropping family photos, turning an existing entertainment center on its side, and painting the walls bright red.

E9: Annapolis, MD: Fox Hollow
Cast: Alex, Genevieve, Laurie, Ty
Gen warms a living room with butterscotch paint, white curtains, framed family pictures, and a combination wood/carpet floor. Laurie enlivens a drab kitchen with muted pumpkin paint, new light fixtures, and a custom pot hanger.

E10: Philadelphia, PA: Strathmore Road
Cast: Alex, Dez, Frank, Amy Wynn
Frank goes earthy by painting a living room brown with a sueding technique. He also creates handmade accents, a child-size tepee, and a window seat with storage. Dez tries for "casual elegance" in a living room, using purple paint, a repeated gray harlequin diamond pattern on the walls, and an end table lamp made out of a trash can.

E11: Philadelphia, PA: Valley Road
Cast: Alex, Doug, Laurie, Amy Wynn
Doug softens a sunroom he names "Blue Lagoon" by painting the walls a deep robin's egg blue, painting blue and white diamonds on the hardwood floor, hanging

Doug's Room
Madison & Forest, Cincinnati, OH

whitewashed bamboo blinds, and adding pale yellow accents. He adds a *Rear Window* touch by placing a pair of binoculars (which he finds in the basement) in the sunroom so the homeowners can watch their children playing outside. Laurie goes Greek, painting a living room deep russet with black and white accents, adding white Grecian urns, and even creating a white bust using one of her homeowners as a model.

E12: Philadelphia, PA: Galahad Road
Cast: Alex, Genevieve, Hildi, Amy Wynn
Hildi warms a family-friendly living/dining room by introducing coffee-color walls, a midnight blue fireplace, a custom-built sectional couch, and zebra-stripe dining chair covers. Gen brightens a basement den by painting the walls lily pad green, adding orange accents, installing a white modern couch, and weaving white fabric on the ceiling to cover the drop-ceiling tiles.

E13: Knoxville, TN: Courtney Oak
Cast: Alex, Frank, Laurie, Amy Wynn
Frank gets in touch with his "inner child" by painting the walls of a basement light denim blue, freehanding murals of trees and flowers, and spray-painting fluffy white clouds. Laurie goes organic by painting a bedroom a deep pistachio green, adding soft draperies, painting a vine around the vanity mirror, and using a cornice board to drape fabric on either side of the headboard.

E14: Cincinnati, OH: Melrose Avenue
Cast: Alex, Frank, Hildi, Ty
Frank adds soft Victorian touches to a living room by exposing the existing wood floor, creating a faux-tin fireplace surround, painting a navy wall border with a rose motif, creating a fireplace screen that matches the border, and building a bench-style coffee table. Hildi gets crafty in a kitchen, creating her own wallpaper with tissue paper and flower stencils based on a fabric pattern. She installs a found dishwasher, extends the countertop, builds an island out of the kitchen table, paints the ceiling and the furniture yellow, and lays vinyl tile flooring.

E15: Cincinnati, OH: Sturbridge Road
Cast: Alex, Doug, Genevieve, Ty
Gen creates an Indian bedroom for a teenage girl by painting the walls with warm golden and red tones,

hanging a beaded curtain, and creating a draped canopy. Doug turns a dining room into a "Zen-Buddhist-Asian room" with a chocolate brown ceiling, warm honey-copper walls, Venetian plaster squares, a distressed wooden dining table, and folded-metal-screen window treatments.

E16: Cincinnati, OH: Madison & Forest
Cast: Alex, Doug, Laurie, Ty
Doug transforms a Victorian living room into an industrial loft with multiple shades of purple paint, a yellow ceiling, custom art made from coordinating paint chips, wall sconces made of candy dishes, and a chair reupholstered in Holstein-print fabric. Laurie warms a tiny bedroom with mustard yellow paint, a custom-built entertainment center, and a short suspended bed canopy.

E17: San Diego, CA: Elm Ridge
Cast: Alex, Genevieve, Hildi, Amy Wynn
In this infamous episode, Gen truly brings the outdoors in: She covers a bedroom wall with Oregon moss, lays a natural-tone tile floor, and adds a canopy that is lit from above with twinkling lights. Hildi works to convince her homeowners that they can brighten a bedroom by painting the walls and furniture black, adding zebra-stripe floor cubes, creating a copper-mesh bust to display in the room, and using exposed subflooring in place of carpet.

E18: San Diego, CA: Hermes Avenue
Cast: Alex, Genevieve, Laurie, Amy Wynn
Laurie brightens a kitchen by painting the walls Tiffany-box blue, installing a wooden slat grid system on one wall, hanging butter yellow draperies, building a banquette seating area, coating the stove in chrome-color paint, and painting the cabinets butter yellow. Gen uses Georgia O'Keeffe's Southwestern paintings as inspiration for transforming a living room. She paints the walls clay red, hangs a cow skull above the fireplace, adds a woven rug, hangs new light fixtures, frames large black and white cropped photos of the homeowners' children, builds a distressed coffee table with firewood legs, and covers the existing baby bumpers with crafts fur.

E19: San Diego, CA: Wilbur Street
Cast: Alex, Doug, Frank, Amy Wynn
Frank mixes British Colonial and tropical looks in a living room with soft mauve paint, exposed wood flooring, several flowerpots and vases, and a custom architectural piece. Doug updates a dark kitchen with a "Tuscan Today" theme, using Venetian plaster tinted "Tuscan Mango" (OK, it's orange), painting the cabinets white and orange, and installing wood flooring.

E20: Knoxville, TN: Stubbs Bluff
Cast: Alex, Doug, Frank, Ty
Doug brings a farmhouse kitchen up-to-date by painting the walls a muted coffee color, adding sage and lilac accents, building benches in the dining area, hanging

silver cooking utensils on the painted cabinet fronts and a shovel and pitchfork painted white on the wall, and laying vinyl tile. He titles his room "Cocteau Country." Frank lets the ideas flow while punching up a basement with a karaoke stage, a tiki hut bar, and several other tropical accents—including a canoe for seating.

E21: Miami, FL: 168th/83rd Streets
Cast: Alex, Dez, Laurie, Ty
Laurie warms up a living room by painting the walls brick red with black and cream accents, building two large bookcases, hanging botanical prints, slipcovering the existing furniture, and using a faux-tortoiseshell finish on a coffee table. Dez adds drama to a bedroom by applying a "pan-Asian ethnic theme" featuring upholstered cornice boards, mosquito netting, and stenciled dragon lampshades.

E22: Fort Lauderdale, FL: 59th Street
Cast: Alex, Frank, Hildi, Ty
Frank adds "comfortable drama" to a living room with bright orange textured walls, a mosaic-top coffee table, slipcovered furniture, and a large custom art project made from three wooden doors. Hildi goes retro in a Fiestaware collector's kitchen by building an acrylic table, adding period chairs, and hanging large globe light fixtures. She also installs a shelving unit to display the homeowner's collection.

E23: Key West, FL: Elizabeth Street
Cast: Alex, Frank, Genevieve, Ty
Frank adds a Caribbean touch to a living room by painting the walls light blue, adding a hand-painted mermaid, building a telephone table, and laying vinyl tiles. Gen makes a tiny living room appear larger with her "Caribbean Chill" design, which includes magenta walls with lime green accents, a large custom-built sectional sofa, and a wall decoupaged with pages torn from a 100-year-old book.

E24: Austin, TX: Wycliff
Cast: Alex, Doug, Hildi, Amy Wynn
Doug creates a funky kitchen by painting the cabinets with blue and purple swirls, extending the existing countertop, applying blue and purple vinyl squares on the wall, and hanging numerous clocks (he titles the room "Time Flies"). Hildi adds drama to a dining room by covering the walls with brown felt, papering the ceiling with small, individual red and gold squares, covering the back of an armoire with dried bamboo leaves, and making custom light fixtures.

E25: Austin, TX: Wing Road
Cast: Alex, Genevieve, Hildi, Amy Wynn
Gen goes south of the border in a kitchen by adding a mosaic tile backsplash, covering the cabinet door insets with textured tin, painting the floors a terra-cotta color, and painting the walls yellow. She also uses colanders as light fixtures and covers a barstool with a tall pasta pot. Hildi brightens a living room by applying a textured glaze over the existing gold paint, covering a wall in wooden squares, sewing silver slipcovers, and adding a cowhide rug.

E26: Austin, TX: Birdhouse Drive
Cast: Alex, Frank, Laurie, Amy Wynn
Frank enlivens a living room by painting three walls sage green, painting the fireplace wall shocking pink, installing floor-to-ceiling shelving on either side of the fireplace, adding a hand-painted checkerboard table, and making unique art pieces. Laurie divides a living/dining room with a suspended piece of fabric, paints the rooms with warm oranges and yellows, adds olive green accents, builds a bench seat, and creates a custom coffee table.

E27: Orlando, FL: Lake Catherine
Cast: Alex, Hildi, Vern, Ty
Vern brings warmth and depth into a wine importer's kitchen by painting the walls with two shades of red, installing a custom-built wine rack, building a new chandelier using 36 wineglasses, and creating a new tabletop. Hildi creates a sleek bedroom with gray walls, an aluminum foil ceiling, gray flannel curtains, bamboo curtain rods, and a black armoire covered in bamboo. She also includes a live canary in her design and names the bird "Hildi."

E28: Orlando, FL: Gotha Furlong
Cast: Alex, Frank, Genevieve, Ty
Gen creates romance in a bedroom by adding a ceiling-height cedar plank headboard, butter yellow paint, throw pillows made from a 1970s tablecloth, and cedar bookshelves. Frank makes a bedroom feel "earthy, arty, and wonderful" by painting the walls tan, adding gauzy white fabric to the four-poster bed, building a cedar window seat with storage drawers, painting a floorcloth, and hand painting batik-print pillows.

E29: Orlando, FL: Winterhaven
Cast: Alex, Doug, Laurie, Ty
Laurie perks up a seldom used living room with yellow paint, sheer window treatments, a geometric wall design, and a large ottoman. Doug regresses to his childhood while decorating a boy's bedroom. Doug's design, "Americana Medley," includes red walls, a blue ceiling, stenciled stars and cow prints, a tree limb headboard, and a barn door window treatment.

E30: Albuquerque, NM: Gloria
Cast: Alex, Doug, Hildi, Ty
Hildi warms up a living room by painting the walls brown and copper, applying yellow fabric paint to the existing furniture, making a curtain rod from copper pipe, and installing an entertainment center. Doug sets sail in a

Laurie's Room
Sam Street, New Jersey

living room ("Wind in Our Sails") by painting the walls slate gray, hanging white curtains, installing a banquette, and suspending a large white canvas from the ceiling.

E31: Santa Fe, NM: Felize
Cast: Alex, Genevieve, Vern, Ty
Gen designs a modern Southwestern living room ("Adobe Mod") by adding white paint, a custom-built sofa, woven-rope end tables, and clay jars. Vern creates a calming oasis in a kitchen by painting the walls pale blue, installing a planter of wheat grass, laying parquet flooring, hanging mirrors, and applying a stained-glass-looking treatment to the cabinet doors.

E32: New Orleans, LA: Jacob Street
Cast: Alex, Hildi, Laurie, Amy Wynn
Laurie creates continuity and flow in a kitchen/office/dining/living room, using pale yellow paint on the walls, a 20-foot-long sisal rug, slipcovers, new kitchen storage, and a new furniture arrangement. Hildi modernizes a kitchen by painting the walls pistachio green, laying black vinyl tile, building a new island, and using plumbing conduit as shelving supports.

E33: New Orleans, LA: Walter Road
Cast: Alex, Frank, Genevieve, Amy Wynn
Gen creates an antique look in a bedroom she titles "Bombay Meets Étouffée." She paints the walls peach and pea green, installs a vintage beaded chandelier, and applies an antiqued gold finish to cornice boards and bookshelves. Frank updates a kitchen by removing garish wallpaper, coating the walls with textured tan paint, painting the cabinet drawers red and green, coiling copper wire around the existing drawer pulls, and installing a large bulletin board to help keep the family organized.

E34: New Orleans, LA: D'evereaux Street
Cast: Alex, Genevieve, Vern, Amy Wynn
Vern kicks up the style in a bedroom shared by two young brothers with a black and white soccer theme. He paints

after ◄

Hildi's Room
James Avenue, Northampton, PA

the walls black and white, upholsters the headboards, creates two desk stations, suspends soccer balls from the ceiling, and lays a black and white vinyl floor complete with a custom soccer ball medallion. Gen heads back to the 1960s in her "Retro Fly" den/guest room by painting multicolor stripes on the walls, hanging retro light fixtures, slipcovering an existing futon, and separating the desk area from the seating area with a chain-link screen.

E35: New York: Shore Road
Cast: Alex, Dez, Genevieve, Amy Wynn
Gen looks to the East for inspiration on a sunporch and creates a tearoom atmosphere with a new sake bar, a seating area, and several organic accents. Dez gives a living room her version of "country with a French twist" by painting the walls yellow, stenciling fern leaves around the room, slipcovering the existing sofa, adding a planter of grass, and hanging geometric window treatments.

E36: New York: Sherwood Drive
Cast: Alex, Doug, Vern, Amy Wynn
Vern creates a serene bedroom by painting the walls lilac-blue, making a television cabinet out of picture frames, hanging yards of indigo-color velvet, installing sconces containing live Beta fish above the bed, and creating a 4-foot-diameter wall clock out of candle sconces and battery-operated clock hands. Doug designs a relaxing "Zen-sational" bedroom by hanging grass cloth on the walls, making light fixtures out of Malaysian baskets, hanging a full-length mirror on an angle, and building a 6-foot-tall fountain.

E37: New York: Linda Court
Cast: Alex, Doug, Frank, Amy Wynn
Doug creates a Mediterranean-flavor living room by covering the walls in yellow Venetian plaster, making custom lamps, building a large armoire to match an existing one, and weaving strips of wood through metal conduit for a woven-wall effect. Frank also heads to the Mediterranean in a living room, applying a faux finish with three shades of

yellow paint, then adding stenciled squares on the walls, a faux fresco created from drywall, and gondola-inspired lamps. He titles his room "Mediterranean Trust Me."

E38: New Jersey: Sam Street
Cast: Alex, Hildi, Laurie, Ty
Laurie warms up a dining room with yellow paint, shades of pink as accents, a custom-built cornice board, and cream paint on the existing furniture. Hildi adds drama and romance to a bedroom by painting the walls a yellowed sage green, bringing in several sage silk fabrics, adding a sofa upholstered in burgundy fabric, extending the existing headboard, and building "pillow pod" seating.

E39: New Jersey: Lincroft
Cast: Alex, Doug, Laurie, Ty
Laurie adds style and function to a small kitchen by laying parquet vinyl flooring, painting the walls an ocher yellow, wall-mounting the microwave oven, painting the cabinets white, and creating a home office/family message center. Doug softens a very red living room by painting the walls sandy taupe, adding wooden strips to accentuate the ceiling height, painting colorful checkerboard designs on coffee tables, sewing several brightly colored rag rugs together to create a large carpet, and designing a wooden candleholder using a rope-and-pulley system. He titles the look "Country Kaleidoscope."

E40: New Jersey: Lafayette Street
Cast: Alex, Frank, Vern, Ty
Frank adds Victorian elements to a dining/living room by painting the walls pink with burgundy accents, showcasing the homeowners' collection of wooden houses, applying decorative molding to the existing entertainment center, and creating original wall art using basic wood-carving skills. Vern creates a baby-friendly living room. He paints the walls two shades of sage green, builds a large upholstered ottoman that doubles as a coffee table, builds a sofa out of a mattress, suspends a mantel for the fireplace, and adds bright blue accents. He also enlarges pictures of the homeowners' baby and uses them as lampshades on three wall lamps.

Season 2

E1: Quakertown, PA: Quakers Way
Cast: Paige, Doug, Hildi, Ty
Doug goes "ball-istic" in a living room, painting the walls lime green, building a custom sofa complete with bowling ball feet, hanging a wall of mirrors, making custom lamps out of gazing balls, and adding brown and blue accents. Hildi introduces viewers to the concept of orthogonal design by painting perpendicular lines on the walls and ceiling of a basement, creating a nine-piece sectional seating area,

hanging three acrylic box frames filled with different types of candy, and screening off a large storage area.

E2: New Jersey: Tall Pines Drive
Cast: Paige, Laurie, Vern, Amy Wynn
Laurie uses several paint colors in a basement to create a large Matisse-inspired mural. She also makes a chalkboard-top kids' table, installs an art station, creates curtains out of place mats, and hangs louvered panels as a room screen. Vern designs a love nest in a bedroom by hanging brown upholstered wall squares, sewing lush draperies using several yards of brown fabric, painting the existing furniture white, installing silver candle chandeliers, and adding new bedside tables.

E3: Maple Glen, PA: Fiedler Road
Cast: Paige, Genevieve, Laurie, Amy Wynn
Laurie paints the walls of a bedroom celadon green, creates a headboard from white and yellow silk squares, paints the existing furniture white, installs bamboo pieces as door hardware, and converts bamboo place mats into pillow shams. Using lillies as inspiration in a living room, Gen paints the walls a yellowed taupe, builds two new couches and a new coffee table, hangs large black and white family photos, and pins prints of vintage botanical postcards to the wall.

E4: Northampton, PA: James Avenue
Cast: Paige, Frank, Hildi, Ty
Hildi updates a living room with mustard-gold paint, aubergine curtains, yellow and red tufted pillows, a sisal rug, silk sunflowers, and a river rock mosaic fireplace. Frank creates a nautical Nantucket theme in a living room by painting the walls pale sage, adding yellow and seafoam green pillows, wrapping rope around the coffee table legs to make the table resemble a pier, and building a dinghy-inspired dog bed.

E5: Providence, RI: Phillips Street
Cast: Paige, Hildi, Vern, Amy Wynn
Hildi adds sophistication to a living room by painting the walls slate gray, making butter yellow slipcovers, adding a touch of charcoal wax to an existing coffee table and side tables, removing the existing ceiling fan, and replacing the drop-ceiling tiles with wood-tone panels. She also creates a child's table with decoupaged drawings of kids holding hands. Vern uses the principles of *feng shui* in a living room by painting the walls and ceiling yellow for wealth, designing a coffee table that holds bamboo stalks for health, attaching small framed mirrors to the ceiling above a candle chandelier, and building a custom fish tank stand for the homeowner's aquarium.

E6: Providence, RI: Wallis Avenue
Cast: Paige, Frank, Genevieve, Amy Wynn
Gen brings a touch of Tuscany to a bedroom by painting the walls sage green, painting the ceiling yellow, installing

floor-to-ceiling shelves, hanging ivy above the headboard, and using light and airy curtains and bed linens. Frank enlivens a kitchen by using several pastel shades of paint, creating a larger tabletop, laying a vinyl floor, and adding painted chevrons to the cabinets.

E7: Boston, MA: Ashfield Street
Cast: Paige, Genevieve, Laurie, Ty
Laurie breathes new life into a bedroom shared by two sisters by painting the walls lavender, creating a trundle bed, painting the existing furniture white, and using ribbons as accents. Gen adds a Moroccan touch to a girl's room by painting the walls and ceiling deep blue, installing a large curtained bed, hanging a Moroccan metal lamp, using gold fabric accents, and hanging white draperies.

E8: Springfield, MA: Sunset Terrace
Cast: Paige, Hildi, Vern, Ty
Hildi creates a Victorian look in a living room by painting the walls light taupe, using blue and white print fabric for draperies and slipcovers, painting blue stripes on the wood floor, sewing a white faux-fur rug, and transforming the fireplace with a custom-built Victorian-style mantelpiece. Vern goes for an even more Victorian look in the other living room by painting the walls yellow to highlight the homeowners' French Provençal furniture, laying a Victorian rug, making a light fixture with silver mesh and hand-strung beads, and creating a custom art piece using celestial and fleur-de-lis stencils.

E9: Boston, MA: Institute Road
Cast: Paige, Doug, Frank, Ty
Doug looks to the leaves for inspiration in his "Autumnal Bliss" bedroom. He papers the walls with bark paper, upholsters the headboard in linen, hangs yellow linen draperies, and frames fall leaves as art. Frank creates a Shakespearean library by painting the walls red, hand painting Elizabethan musician cutouts for the walls, and painting a rounded-stone pattern on the floor.

Vern's Room
Fairway Court, Maryland

after ◄

E10: Philadelphia, PA: Jeannes Street
Cast: Paige, Genevieve, Vern, Amy Wynn
Gen turns a basement den into a 3-D Scrabble board by painting taupe and white grids on the floors and ceiling, installing a black wall-length bar, making pillows that mimic Scrabble board squares, and framing game boards to hang on the wall. Vern uses the female homeowner's love of the holiday season for inspiration in a living room by painting the walls and ceiling deep red, making camel slipcovers and draperies, and building a dark wood armoire with mirrored doors.

E11: New Jersey: Perth Road
Cast: Paige, Frank, Laurie, Amy Wynn
Frank gives a living room a homier feel by adding light camel paint, a coffee table topped with a picture frame, textured folk art on the wall, and a custom-built armoire ("It's kind of a puppet theater cathedral"). Laurie redoes a bedroom without altering the existing Queen Anne furniture. She paints the walls a warm apricot, builds a custom canopy that rests on top of the four-poster bed, and adds bookshelves as nightstands.

E12: Maryland: Village Green
Cast: Paige, Doug, Genevieve, Amy Wynn
Gen refines a bedroom by painting one wall chocolate brown, covering the ceiling with gold metallic paint, installing a custom geometric shelving unit, making a fountain, decoupaging sewing patterns to a wall, and creating a light fixture out of a large wicker ball. Doug creates an elegant and sophisticated "Strip Stripe" look in a bedroom by painting the walls gray, building a large upholstered headboard with storage in the back, painting the furniture white, and painting large Matisse-inspired figures directly on the wall.

E13: Maryland: Fairway Court
Cast: Paige, Doug, Vern, Amy Wynn
Vern softens a bedroom by painting the walls a light gray, hanging charcoal draperies, suspending a canopy over the existing sleigh bed, and dangling 100 clear crystals from the canopy edge. Doug designs a fantasy bedroom suite for train enthusiasts by rounding the ceiling edges, covering the walls with blue paint and fabric, and building fake walls and windows to mimic the inside of a Pullman car.

E14: Chicago, IL: Edward Road
Cast: Paige, Frank, Laurie, Ty
Frank adds an aged-copper look to a kitchen by using touches of terra-cotta, copper, and green paint. He also lays earth-tone vinyl flooring, paints a faux-tile backsplash, makes a large floorcloth, and adds a butcher-block island. Laurie gives a living room a touch of European flair by painting a faux-fresco finish in yellow tones, installing dark wooden beams on the ceiling, hanging burlap draperies, painting a faux-inlay top on an occasional table, and repeating an X motif throughout the room.

E15: Chicago, IL: Spaulding Avenue
Cast: Paige, Doug, Hildi, Ty
Doug adds a little funk to a living room by painting the walls yellow, using Venetian plaster to make black and yellow blocks on a wall, upholstering the furniture with zebra-print fabric, and suspending a tabletop from the ceiling to create a dining area. Hildi brings the outdoors into a bedroom. She paints the walls cream and the trim a deep plum and then draws large "swooshes" of grass on the walls with chalk pastels. She adds a row of grass planter boxes along one wall, uses bursts of orange in pillows, and installs a large wooden bed.

E16: Chicago, IL: Fairview Avenue
Cast: Paige, Genevieve, Vern, Ty
Vern brightens a kitchen by painting the walls pear green, painting the cabinets white, creating a new cabinet for storage, making a new table, laying a black and white geometric rug, upholstering a storage bench that doubles as seating at the table, and hanging upholstered cushions against the wall above the bench. Gen gives the lodge look to a basement living room by painting the walls cinnamon, installing a pine plank ceiling, hanging wood wainscoting, slipcovering the furniture, and highlighting the fireplace with built-in shelves.

E17: Colorado: Berry Avenue
Cast: Paige, Genevieve, Hildi, Amy Wynn
Gen paints the walls of a kitchen bright eggplant, paints the cabinets vanilla-sage, removes the center panels of the cabinet doors to showcase the dishes inside, and prints each family member's face on a chair cover for personalized seating. Hildi creates an intimate living room by painting the walls a deep chocolate brown, using sage fabrics, transforming the coffee table into a large ottoman, and installing a wall-size fountain made to mimic the shape of the existing windows.

E18: Colorado: Cherry Street
Cast: Paige, Genevieve, Laurie, Amy Wynn
Gen gives a living room a punch of personality by painting the walls brick red with sage accents, hanging antlers on the walls, installing floor-to-ceiling shelving, making a focal point out of one of the homeowners' landscape photos, and creating an inlaid rug. Laurie applies a touch of mod to a living room by painting gray and yellow horizontal stripes on the walls, building a new glass-top coffee table, hanging silver silk draperies, and adding a piece of custom artwork.

E19: Colorado: Andes Way
Cast: Paige, Frank, Vern, Amy Wynn
Frank creates a family-friendly living room by rag-rolling the walls with cream and peach paint, hanging valances coated with brown builder's paper, building a white and sage armoire, and creating a kids' nook with a large art table, plant murals on the walls, and wooden clouds nailed to the ceiling. Vern stripes a living room, laying

two colors of laminate flooring in alternating stripes, painting a red horizontal stripe on the khaki walls, and continuing the same stripe across the draperies.

E20: Colorado: Stoneflower Drive
Cast: Paige, Doug, Frank, Amy Wynn
Frank injects some whimsy into a bedroom by painting the walls celadon green, building a large headboard that mimics a skyline, creating a matching dog bed, and hanging gold curtains. Doug updates a living room with a design he calls "Smoke Screen." He paints the walls moss green, removes colonial molding, adds pewter accents, hangs pleated metal screening, and builds screen doors to cover shelving around the fireplace.

E21: Seattle, WA: 137th Street
Cast: Paige, Doug, Frank, Ty
Doug does "Denim Deluxe" in a living room. He paints a white grid pattern on chocolate walls, slipcovers the furniture with brown and ivory denim, makes art pieces with brightly colored tissue paper, lowers the existing coffee table, installs white wainscoting, and builds a white facade to cover the brick fireplace. Frank brightens a living room by painting the walls reddish orange and yellow, installing a new mantel, hanging shelves on either side of the fireplace, making a fireplace screen painted with folk art characters, and creating a window valance with place mats and clothespins.

E22: Seattle, WA: Dakota Street
Cast: Paige, Laurie, Vern, Ty
Vern adds drama and romance to a living room by painting the walls golden yellow, hanging brown draperies, building an armoire with red upholstered door panels, slipcovering the furniture in white fabric dyed with tea bags, and constructing red candle torchères. Laurie tries to convince her homeowners that she can warm up a bedroom with parchment-color paint, soft white and blue fabrics, various chocolate brown accents on the furniture and headboard, and painted partition screens.

E23: Seattle, WA: 56th Place
Cast: Paige, Genevieve, Hildi, Ty
Hildi entirely covers a basement rec room in magenta and taupe fabric hung from the ceiling. She also builds new coffee and side tables and slipcovers new sofas with magenta fabric. Gen creates an Asian living room, using shimmery silver and red paints and coating one wall in a metal paint that oxidizes to a rusted finish. She makes a valance out of an obi and uses cedar flowerpots as picture frames.

E24: Oregon: Alyssum Avenue
Cast: Paige, Genevieve, Hildi, Amy Wynn
Hildi creates a cozy bedroom by upholstering the walls and ceiling with silver-blue fabric, building a bed from storage cubes, draping sheer white fabric from the ceiling center over the bed corners, hanging a chandelier above

Frank's Room
Alsea Court, Oregon

the bed, and adding a blue monogram to white bed linens. Gen adds a graphic touch to a living room by painting the walls bright yellow, covering a wall with 6-inch wooden squares, building cedar shelving under the stairs, and hanging clotheslines to display art and photos.

E25: Oregon: Alsea Court
Cast: Paige, Frank, Laurie, Amy Wynn
Frank goes south of the border in a kitchen by painting a serape on the ceiling, making a basket-weave wall treatment with sheet metal strips, painting the cabinet door center panels silver, designing a distressed tabletop, and upholstering dining chairs with serape fabric. Laurie brings warmth to a living room by painting the walls amber, using several expensive fabrics in warm harvest shades, building a long armoire with gold filigree door insets, and designing a large central ottoman.

E26: Portland, OR: Everett Street
Cast: Paige, Doug, Vern, Amy Wynn
Doug transforms a family room into an Art Deco theater by painting the floors and ceiling chocolate brown, covering the walls with chocolate brown fabric, building graduated platforms for silver chairs, suspending the television from the ceiling, and installing aisle lights. Vern creates a cohesive look in a living/dining room by painting the walls sage green and hanging sage draperies with white satin stripes on the windows and the walls of the dining area. He also builds a custom armoire and buffet with square wooden insets stained various colors and creates a custom lampshade with handmade art paper.

E27: Santa Clara, CA: Lafayette Street
Cast: Paige, Frank, Laurie, Ty
Frank adds a festive touch to the living room of a Delta Gamma residence by painting the walls two shades of a peachy orange; highlighting the curved ceiling with stenciled stars, triangles, swirls, and dots; painting the sorority letters above the fireplace; and installing a window bench seat. Laurie updates the Delta Gamma chapter room by painting the walls a muted seafoam, stenciling yellow anchors on the walls, designing a coffee table with hidden additional seating, and making a candelabra out of a captain's wheel.

E28: California: Corte Rosa
Cast: Paige, Laurie, Vern, Ty
Vern gives a bedroom an exotic resort decor by painting the walls light chino, upholstering the bedside tabletops with faux leather, adding tribal- and safari-print fabrics to the draperies and bed linens, hanging a red glass light fixture, and building storage cabinets on a large plant ledge. Laurie creates romance in a bedroom by painting the walls sage green, hanging a French tester canopy above the bed, painting the existing furniture mocha brown, installing a window seat with storage cabinets, and hanging dark green draperies.

E29: California: Grenadine Way
Cast: Paige, Frank, Vern, Ty
Vern looks to vintage Indian fabrics for inspiration in a bedroom. He paints the walls soft blue, lays wood laminate flooring, installs a large headboard of basket-woven iridescent fabric, and hangs amber glass candleholders. Frank gives ethnic flair to a living room by painting a mantel with stripes of mustard, white, taupe, and black; designing a large wooden sculpture; and building a new coffee table, armoire, and cornice box.

E30: Berkeley, CA: Prospect Street
Cast: Paige, Doug, Genevieve, Ty
Doug cleans up the Delta Upsilon fraternity chapter room (and goes "DU-clectic") by painting the walls lime green, installing bench seating, constructing two huge circular ottomans upholstered with lime and orange fabrics, and suspending a tabletop from the ceiling. Gen adds classic Hollywood-style glamour to the Alpha Omicron Pi sorority chapter room by painting white and silver stripes on the walls, adding black and silver throw pillows, building a large armoire, and commissioning her team to trace silhouettes of Paige and herself for wall art.

E31: Oakland, CA: Webster Street
Cast: Paige, Genevieve, Hildi, Amy Wynn
Hildi covers the walls of a living room with straw. She also installs a wall of bookshelves, covers the fireplace with copper mesh and glass rods, applies pink textured plaster to the ceiling, and screens the windows with wooden louvered blinds. Gen brightens a kitchen by

painting the cabinets yellow and the walls cobalt blue, building a tile-top island and kids' table, personalizing dishware with family art and photos, and designing a backlit display shelf for a glass bottle collection.

E32: California: Peralta Street
Cast: Paige, Doug, Hildi, Amy Wynn
Hildi divides a living room into quadrants by painting two opposite corners of the room and ceiling silver and painting the remaining corners and ceiling space violet. She supplements the look with a clear-glass mosaic on the fireplace surround, four industrial-style chairs, and a large circular ottoman upholstered in silver and violet. Doug thinks pink in a dining room. He paints the walls bubble gum pink, paints the ceiling chocolate brown, hangs a lamp upside down from the ceiling, upholsters new white dining chairs with lime green T-shirts, and tops new storage units with green gazing balls.

E33: Los Angeles, CA: Willoughby Avenue
Cast: Paige, Doug, Genevieve, Ty
Doug sees red in a living room: He stencils the walls and doors in red and white, using a rectangular graphic based on an existing pillow pattern. He paints the ceiling gray, lays a red shag rug, and builds a U-shape couch with red upholstery. Gen designs a swingin' living room with 1950s flair by painting the walls aqua, disguising stains on the wood floor by painting it black, transforming mod place mats into wall sconces, slipcovering a futon in white vinyl, and laying a bookcase on its side to create a new coffee table.

E34: Los Angeles, CA: Springdale Drive
Cast: Paige, Laurie, Vern, Ty
Vern brightens a dining room by painting the walls yellow, hanging bronze draperies, installing a wall-length buffet with built-in storage, and designing a multiarmed halogen chandelier with gold vellum shades and a hanging candleholder. Laurie enlivens a basement den by painting the walls yellow, slipcovering the existing furniture with natural cotton duck fabric, sewing an aqua Roman shade,

installing several yellow and aqua shadow box shelves, designing a folding screen to mask exercise equipment, and painting squares and rectangles in various shades of aqua to create custom wall art.

E35: California: Abbeywood Lane
Cast: Paige, Frank, Hildi, Ty
Frank gives a living room a cohesive look by painting the walls sage green; building an upholstered wall hanging in shades of peach, coral, and yellow; painting a life-size image of the homeowners' toddler on the wall; making throw pillows out of fabric designed by the homeowner; and crafting candleholders out of 4x4s covered with license plates. Hildi creates her version of a nautical living room by painting the walls black, nailing 120 lightly stained 1x2s on the walls in a vertical arrangement about 2 inches apart, building two large mirror-image couches upholstered in seafoam fabric, creating seafoam throw pillows and draperies, and mounting photos of the ocean onto blocks of wood.

E36: Austin, TX: La Costa Drive (Celebrity Episode)
Cast: Paige, Hildi, Vern, Ty
In the first celebrity episode of *Trading Spaces*, Vern breathes life into the bonus room of Dixie Chicks lead vocalist Natalie Maines. Vern paints the walls yellow; installs a wall-length desk and sewing unit; hangs a huge chandelier; and sews throw pillows, draperies, and bed linens with shimmery red fabric. Hildi adds style to a sewing room, which belongs to Natalie's mother, by railroading gray and sage fabric on the walls, installing wooden louvered wall dividers, building a 14-foot-long couch, reupholstering a vintage shampoo chair with sage chenille, and covering a coffee table with slate tiles.

E37: Texas: Sherwood Street
Cast: Paige, Frank, Genevieve, Amy Wynn
Frank transforms a kitchen by removing strawberry-print wallpaper, sponge-painting a focal-point wall, hanging new draperies with a pear motif, painting faux tiles on the avocado green floor and countertops, and hanging a thin plywood sunburst around the existing fluorescent light. Gen conjures a New England cottage feel in a bedroom by painting three of the walls pale smoke-gray, painting one of the walls ultrabright white, building a fireplace mantel-style

Gen's Room
George Road, Maine

headboard, creating curtain tiebacks from red neckties, sewing bed pillows from pinstriped suit jackets, distressing the existing ceiling fan blades, and adding a reading nook.

E38: Houston, TX: Sawdust Street
Cast: Paige, Doug, Laurie, Amy Wynn
Laurie refines a living room by painting the walls margarine yellow, building a wall-length bookshelf, hanging bamboo blinds and yellow drapery panels, and adding two spicy orange chairs. Doug goes "Zen/Goth" in a living room by painting the walls blood red, building an L-shape couch, hanging a large wrought-iron light fixture, adding a black faux-fur rug, and enlarging a photo of the female homeowner in lingerie and knee-high boots to hang over the fireplace.

E39: Houston, TX: Appalachian Trail
Cast: Paige, Doug, Laurie, Amy Wynn
Laurie adds style to an office/playroom by painting the walls terra-cotta, building a large shelving and desk unit with plumbing conduit, painting the existing coffee table and armoire in cream and black, adding new seating, and creating the illusion of symmetry with cream draperies on an off-center window. Doug goes for a soft look in a bedroom by painting the walls pale blue, upholstering a tall headboard in blue chenille, sewing new blue and white bed linens, and installing custom light fixtures. He titles the room "A Pretty Room by Doug."

E40: Plano, TX: Bent Horn Court
Cast: Paige, Genevieve, Vern, Ty
Gen gets in touch with her inner child as she designs a playroom, painting multicolor polka dots on the walls, cutting movable circles of green outdoor carpeting for the floors, building a large castle-shape puppet theater, hanging fabric-covered tire swings, and designing four upholstered squares on wheels with storage space inside. Vern gets in touch with his rustic side in a living room by laying natural-color adhesive carpet tiles, painting an existing armoire and other furniture pieces black, and building a combination ottoman/coffee table/bench unit.

Hildi's Room
Shady Valley Road, Plano, TX

Laurie's Room
Springdale Drive, Los Angeles, CA

E41: Plano, TX: Shady Valley Road
Cast: Paige, Doug, Hildi, Ty

Hildi creates a two-tone bedroom by painting the walls bright white, installing 12-inch orange baseboards, building new head- and footboards that match the pitch of the cathedral ceiling and slipcovering them in white, and upholstering a chair with white faux fur. Doug adds sophisticated style to a playroom by painting the wall moss green ("Moss Madness"), installing beams on the ceiling in a barnlike formation, building a basket-weave armoire, revamping a futon into a daybed, and hanging bifold doors on a toy closet.

E42: Texas: Sutton Court
Cast: Paige, Frank, Laurie, Ty

Laurie designs a kitchen, using the homeowners' china for inspiration. She paints the walls taupe with white trim, builds large wooden shadow boxes to display china pieces, hangs new light fixtures, and uses taupe fabric for the window treatments and chair cushions. Frank works with a Southwest theme in a living room, adding chamois-cloth accents to the existing furniture, building a footstool out of a saddle, hanging several custom-made art pieces, designing a Mission-style armoire, and making potted "cactus" out of vegetables.

E43: Raleigh, NC: Legging Lane
Cast: Paige, Frank, Hildi, Amy Wynn

Hildi adds romance to a bedroom by painting the walls slate gray, hanging smoky plum draperies, sewing a tufted lavender coverlet, framing a favorite picture of the Eiffel Tower, and building cubic bench seats and nightstands. Frank lets his creativity flow in a playroom by painting the walls, furniture, doors, and floors in a multitude of pastel colors. He also hides a large refrigerator, builds an armoire to house media equipment, and designs a large toy chest.

E44: North Carolina: Southerby Drive
Cast: Paige, Doug, Hildi, Amy Wynn

Doug adds an Eastern touch to a bedroom by painting the walls china blue and painting white chinoiserie murals. He builds a black four-poster bed with PVC pipe, adds a custom-built sculpture, hangs white draperies, and paints the furniture black. He aptly titles his room "China Blue." Hildi also displays Eastern influences in a bedroom, painting the walls a soft green and installing a wall of shoji screens to create a headboard. She covers the screens and the existing furniture with a lavender crackle finish, hangs lavender draperies, and upholsters a sofa with purple fabric.

E45: Wake Forest, NC: Rodney Bay
Cast: Paige, Laurie, Vern, Amy Wynn

Vern adds drama to a bedroom by painting the walls gray, attaching a fabric canopy to the ceiling, designing a headboard with interior lights that shine out of the top, painting the existing furniture black, and upholstering a chair with gray flannel. Laurie brightens a living room by painting the walls a bold shade of green, installing two floor-to-ceiling shelving units with crown molding, hanging yellow draperies, adding several pillows in warm harvest shades to the existing off-white sofa, and hanging a new parchment-shade light fixture.

E1: Maine: George Road
Cast: Paige, Doug, Genevieve, Ty

Doug adds warmth to a kitchen by painting the walls umber, painting the woodwork white, installing a butcher-block countertop, building a large pantry unit with bifold doors, and sewing a large tablecloth. Gen updates a dark kitchen by painting the walls bright green, installing a black and white tile countertop, building a butcher-block island, hanging wood laminate wall paneling, and installing a 1930s-style light fixture.

E2: Portland, OR: Rosemont Avenue
Cast: Paige, Laurie, Vern, Ty

Laurie goes nautical in a living room by painting the walls deep aqua blue, painting the fireplace white, putting a cream-tone paint wash on wooden chairs and upholstering them with zebra-print fabric, and installing a vintage mercury glass chandelier. Vern brightens a living room by painting the walls yellow, hanging black and yellow Roman shades, installing French doors, covering the ceiling with white steel squares, hanging a ceiling fan, using black slipcovers for the existing furniture, and adding silver fold-up trays to serve as side tables and a coffee table.

E3: Maine: Joseph Drive
Cast: Paige, Frank, Laurie, Ty

Laurie enlivens a bedroom by painting the walls soft yellow, building an Asian-style shelving unit, designing a new headboard, sewing gray and white toile bedding, and adding an unusual floral light fixture. Frank shows another side of his design style in a bachelor's bedroom: He paints the walls and ceiling dark blue-green, hangs simple white draperies, sews a large plastic envelope to hold a pencil drawing of a leaf on the wall, builds a table that houses three wooden bins, and adds pet collars to a rocking chair.

E4: Long Island, NY: Steuben Boulevard
Cast: Paige, Edward, Frank, Ty

Edward jazzes up a bedroom by painting the walls light mocha, hanging wall sconces, building an Art Deco armoire, painting Deco patterns on the closet doors, installing lights around the bottom edge of the bed frame, hanging a canopy, and painting a faux-malachite finish on the furniture tops and wall sconces. Frank gets woodsy in a dining room, painting the walls deep orange, installing pine doors between the dining room and kitchen, creating a coffee table out of a large flowerpot, painting white birch trees all around the room, and making a large pig-topped weather vane to sit above the fireplace.

E5: Long Island, NY: Split Rock Road
Cast: Paige, Genevieve, Vern, Amy Wynn

Gen brightens a dark kitchen by painting the walls white, the trim celadon green, the window shutters pale blue, and the cabinets yellow. She also polishes the existing copper stove hood, hangs white wooden slats on one wall, builds a butcher-block table, skirts the dining chairs in white fabric, and coats a new light fixture with copper spray paint. Her design is inspired by a sea-glass necklace the homeowner wears nearly every day. Vern adds a soft touch to a kitchen by painting the walls and cabinet door insets green, painting parts of the cabinet doors white, stenciling white fleurs-de-lis on the cabinet doors, building a new laminate countertop, laying a two-tone parquet floor, using green toile fabrics on Roman shades and table linens, adding touches of green gingham to the tablecloth, and adding several green-shaded table lamps to the countertop.

E6: New York: Whitlock Road
Cast: Paige, Doug, Genevieve, Amy Wynn

Gen designs a bedroom with an espresso color scheme: She paints the walls café au lait, uses darker java on the ceiling beams, and paints sections of the ceiling cream. She also sews orange asterisks on a white bedspread, builds a combination headboard/desk, and exposes original wood flooring. Doug updates a bedroom by painting squares on the wall in multiple shades of sage, building a mantel-like headboard, designing S-shape side tables, sewing stripes of yarn on a white bedspread, and framing strips of wood veneer for bedside art. He titles the room "Don't Box Me In."

E7: New York: Half Hollow Turn
Cast: Paige, Frank, Kia, Amy Wynn

Frank updates a living room by painting the walls bamboo yellow, adding black accents on the walls and the furniture, using concrete stepping-stones to create side tables, converting a garden bench into a coffee table, and hanging a custom sculpture made from electrical and plumbing components. Kia gets funky in a basement rec room by painting the walls purple and light green, building a wall-length bench with purple velvet upholstery, hanging a swirly purple wallpaper border, installing halogen lights on a running cable, and creating green draperies.

E8: Philadelphia, PA: 22nd Street
Cast: Paige, Edward, Genevieve, Ty

Edward adds ethnic flair to a living room by painting the walls red, texturing the fireplace with black paint and tissue paper, hanging an existing rug on the wall, building a chaise lounge with finial feet, and installing an entertainment center made of shadow boxes. Gen heads to Cuba in a bedroom by covering the walls with white textured paint, adding a faux-wood grain finish to the doors, building a headboard enhanced with a blown-up image from a Cuban cigar box, designing lighted plastic bed tables, and creating picture frames out of cigar boxes.

E9: Philadelphia, PA: Gettysburg Lane
Cast: Paige, Frank, Vern, Ty
Frank updates a kitchen by painting the walls and cabinets several different colors, laying a stone-look vinyl tile, installing a new countertop, adding decorative elements to a half-wall to create a new serving bar, and mounting plates with wooden food cutouts across the soffit. Vern adds his version of cottage style to a living room by painting the walls yellow, installing white wainscoting, building a 12-foot-wide shelving and storage unit, framing large copies of old family photos, making a "quilt" of images to hang above the storage unit, and adding touches of denim fabric throughout the room.

E10: Pennsylvania: Gorski Lane
Cast: Paige, Doug, Frank, Ty
Frank adds a celestial touch in a bedroom by painting the ceiling deep plum and painting silver stars across it. He paints the walls with several shades of cream and green, adds small blocks of color to the paneled doors, builds a writing desk, hangs a small cabinet upside down on the wall, installs a ceiling fan, and makes several pieces of custom artwork. Doug brings some "jungle boogie" to a bedroom by painting zebra stripes across all four walls, painting the ceiling dark brown, suspending a bamboo grid from the ceiling, building a breakfast table and chairs from scavenged lumber, and covering the existing headboard with sticks and bamboo.

E11: Long Island, NY: Dover Court
Cast: Paige, Edward, Vern, Amy Wynn
Vern sets a boy's bedroom in motion by painting the walls various shades of blue, building a race car bed with working headlights, suspending a working train track and toy planes from the ceiling, hanging a motorcycle swing made from recycled tires, and hanging precut letters on the walls to spell out words like "woosh" and "zoom." Edward brings the outdoors into a bedroom by painting the walls moss green and antiquing a landscape print above the bed. He alters prefab side tables with filigreelike cuts, disguises the existing lamps with black spray paint and fabric slipcovers, hangs antique glass shutters over the windows, and builds a large entertainment center using the existing side tables and more glass shutters.

E12: Pennsylvania: Victoria Drive
Cast: Paige, Doug, Kia, Amy Wynn
Doug creates a cabin feel in a living room by covering the walls in soft brown-tinted Venetian plaster, hanging red Roman shades, covering a ready-made coffee table with leather, staining the existing sofa and coffee tables a darker color, sewing cow-print throw pillows, building a large armoire covered with rough-cut poplar, and hanging leftover lumber on the walls in decorative stripes. Kia creates her version of an indoor garden in a guest bedroom by painting the walls yellow, hanging a flowery wallpaper border on the ceiling, creating a duvet from synthetic turf and silk flowers, building a headboard from a tree limb, hanging a chair swing from a cedar arbor, placing gravel under the swing, and building a picket fence room divider.

E13: New Jersey: Manitoba Trail
Cast: Paige, Doug, Frank, Amy Wynn
Frank goes all out in a country living/dining room by painting the walls light green, distressing the wood floors, painting a faux rug beneath the coffee table, applying several decorative paint colors and finishes to an antique cabinet, building custom lamps with large antique yarn spools, and creating three homemade country-girl dolls with pillow forms. Doug brightens a living room by painting everything—the walls, ceiling, ceiling beams, fireplace, and ceiling fans—bright white ("White Whoa"). He buys two new white sofas, hangs bright blue draperies, installs a new doorbell that blends into the white wall, sews many brightly colored throw pillows, makes a large framed mirror, and creates custom art pieces.

E14: Nazareth, PA: First Street
Cast: Paige, Doug, Vern, Amy Wynn
Vern adds a touch of serenity to a living room by painting three walls taupe and one wall deep blue, adding a new mantel, sewing throw pillows with a wave-motif fabric, suspending mini symbiotic environments from the ceiling, building a coffee table with a center inset of sand and candles, and placing six fountains around the fireplace. Doug gives a kitchen an earthy feel by laying brown peel-and-stick vinyl flooring, painting the walls beige, installing new orange laminate countertops, painting the cabinets yellow with an orange glaze, adding crown molding to the cabinet tops, building a pie safe, and upholstering the dining chairs with red-orange fabric.

E15: New Jersey: Catania Court
Cast: Paige, Genevieve, Hildi, Amy Wynn
Hildi has the golden touch in a bedroom: She paints the walls yellow-green, sews bedding with fabrics she purchased in India, uses batik-inspired stamps to create gold accents on the ceiling and around the room, replaces the existing baseboards with taller ones, adds a gold wash to the existing furniture, builds a low-slung "opium couch," and hangs a vintage glass light fixture. Gen finds the silver lining in a dining room: She paints the walls orange-red, hangs silver crown molding, paints the trim and chair rail ivory, hangs ivory and silver draperies, paints

Vern's Room
Gettysburg Lane,
Philadelphia, PA

after

after

Gen's Room
Quebec Place, Washington, D.C.

a canvas floorcloth to lay under the table, and hangs a new light fixture that has small tree limbs attached to it.

E16: Philadelphia, PA: East Avenue
Cast: Paige, Frank, Hildi, Amy Wynn
Hildi gets graphic in a living room by painting three walls yellow, covering one wall with a large Lichtenstein-inspired portrait of herself, adding a glass-shelf bar area, building all new tables and chairs, sewing cushions with mod pink and orange fabric, and re-covering a thrift store couch with red fabric. Frank brightens a living room by painting the walls deep purple, painting the ceiling bright red, designing a coffee table unit with four bases that move apart and become extra seating, and creating wall art with rain gutter materials and round wooden cutouts.

E17: Virginia: Gentle Heights Court
Cast: Paige, Hildi, Kia, Ty
Hildi sets up camp in a boy's bedroom by painting the walls and ceiling midnight blue, hanging a moon-shape light fixture, placing glow-in-the-dark stars on the ceiling, hanging a solar system mobile, building a 13-foot-tall rock climbing wall, adding several pieces of fold-up camping furniture, placing the mattress in a room-size tent, using a blue sleeping bag as a duvet, and placing camping lanterns around the room. Kia adds sensuous details to a bedroom by painting the walls orange and the trim Grecian blue, hanging a red and gold wallpaper border, creating a Taj Mahal cutout to place around the existing entertainment center, installing two wooden columns from India, adding bedding made from sari fabrics, and suspending the bed from the ceiling with chains.

E18: Arlington, VA: First Road
Cast: Paige, Doug, Hildi, Ty
Hildi gift-wraps a bedroom by painting the walls Tiffany-box aqua blue, adding a duvet and Roman shades in the same aqua blue, airbrushing white "ribbons" on the walls

and fabrics, hanging white lamps with square shades above the headboard, building acrylic side tables that light up from inside, and adding bright silver accents. Doug warms up a bedroom by painting the walls and ceiling a deep gray-blue; hanging white Roman shades, brown silk curtains, and cornice boards; constructing a headboard from a large existing window frame; balancing the headboard with a new armoire that features white silk door insets; and creating custom artwork in brown and navy. He titles the room "Framed."

E19: Washington, D.C.: Quebec Place
Cast: Paige, Genevieve, Vern, Ty
Gen dishes up a serene living room inspired by her favorite Thai soup. She paints the walls a light bone color and gives the room lemongrass green accents, a newly constructed sofa, a wall-length valance with lemongrass curtains, and lotus flower light fixtures. Vern turns up the heat in a newlywed couple's bedroom by painting the fireplace and dressing room red, installing a floor-to-ceiling mirrored wall in the dressing area, hanging rows of crystals above the fireplace, sewing red silk Roman shades, and installing a large headboard with red silk insets.

E20: Indiana: River Valley Drive
Cast: Paige, Doug, Genevieve, Amy Wynn
Gen tones down a brightly colored living room by painting the walls a sleek silver-gray, painting the existing furniture white, designing a new entertainment center made out of stacked white boxes with punched-aluminum door insets, and adding a few bold touches of color with green curtains, a new green room screen, and a fuchsia ottoman. Doug puts his foot down in his "Back from Brazil" living room, hanging a three-section painting of his own foot. He also stencils white flowers—inspired by sarongs—on the walls, slipcovers the existing furniture in white, highlights the fireplace mantel with a large vertical wooden extension, designs an acrylic light fixture, and sews throw pillows from tie-dyed sarongs.

E21: Indiana: Fieldhurst Lane
Cast: Paige, Doug, Vern, Amy Wynn
Doug gets back to his Midwestern roots in a bedroom by painting the walls orange, installing wainscoting upholstered with tan fabric, creating custom paintings of wheat and corn, embellishing simple white bedding with orange ribbon and yarn, and designing a large armoire. Vern sets a restful scene in a bedroom by painting the walls a light blue, attaching oak plywood squares to a wall, painting the existing furniture black, reupholstering a chaise lounge with dark blue velvet, hanging blue velvet draperies, wrapping the bed frame with white beaded garland, and installing new sconces and a ceiling fixture with white beaded shades.

E22: Indianapolis, IN: Halleck Way
Cast: Paige, Edward, Kia, Amy Wynn
Edward designs a soft yet masculine bedroom by painting the tray ceiling slate blue and white, painting the walls and existing furniture tan, hanging a customized light fixture with a hand-painted glass frame, draping white fabric across the length of one wall, hanging brown draperies made from lush fabrics, and slipcovering the head- and footboards. He also rearranges the furniture and creates neoclassic wall shelves. Kia walks like an Egyptian in a bedroom by painting the walls "Tut Wine" and "Pharaoh Gold," building pyramid-shape cornice boards, and hanging framed Egyptian prints and a handmade Eye of Horus. She also paints a personalized hieroglyphic message for the homeowners ("David loves Noel") on an existing room screen and installs a ceiling fan with palm leaves attached to the blades.

E23: Missouri: Sunburst Drive
Cast: Paige, Genevieve, Vern, Ty
Gen draws inspiration for a bedroom from gauchos

(Argentine cowboys): She paints the walls deep brown, creates faux crown molding by bringing the ceiling paint several inches down onto the walls, installs a woven leather-and-red-velvet headboard, and glues pictures of gauchos to the closet doors. She also builds an upholstered bench and pulls in furniture from other rooms that matches the room's color scheme. Vern adds a masculine edge to a girlie bedroom by painting the walls soft blue, painting the existing furniture and doors red, designing a wall-length desk and computer hutch, installing a headboard made of upholstered leather squares, and adding several wrought-iron light fixtures and Moroccan-inspired accents.

E24: Scott Air Force Base, MO: Ash Creek
Cast: Paige, Doug, Kia, Ty
Doug travels down Route 66 in a child's bedroom by laying gray carpet, painting highway stripes and road signs on the walls, and installing a front and back end from two actual cars. (He adds a mattress in the back end of one car, and the front end of the other car serves as a toy chest.) Kia creates "Military Chic" in a living/dining room, using various shades of gray paint, new chair rails, a gray and white camouflage wallpaper border, pillows and cushions in the same camouflage color combination, a new storage bench, a faux fireplace, a red slipcover, red decorative accents, and draperies made from a gray parachute.

E25: Missouri: Sweetbriar Lane
Cast: Paige, Edward, Frank, Ty
Edward designs a sleek bedroom by painting the walls shades of gray, white, and China blue; adding extra closet and storage space; and designing a mirrored entertainment armoire to conceal the TV. He also hangs a light fixture wrapped in pearls; adds gray, purple, blue, and green fabrics; and creates a sculpture from curled metal. Frank creates an eclectic bedroom, painting the walls orange and installing large eyes made of copper tubing above the bed. An upholstered lip headboard completes the face, and a new platform bed stands beneath it. Frank paints the fireplace purple and creates an artistic theme by attaching a giant pencil on one wall and painting female figures near it to look as though they'd been sketched.

E26: London, England: Garden Flat
Cast: Paige, Genevieve, Hildi, Handy Andy
Gen enlivens a bedroom by painting the walls a rich, spicy orange, painting a small alcove red, and hanging many yellow-green draperies. She also builds a new platform bed with drawers beneath, adds a ready-made dresser, creates closet space along one wall, installs crown molding, and hangs rows of framed Chinese newsprint. Hildi brightens a bedroom shared by two girls by splattering brightly colored paint onto white walls, laying fluffy white carpet, framing the girls' artwork, and sewing rainbow-color draperies. She also installs doors

Kia's Room
Halleck Way, Indianapolis, IN

Edward's Room
Sweetbriar Lane, Missouri

on an existing wall-size shelving unit, builds beds and nightstands on casters, and creates a "secret garden" area with wheat grass plants.

E27: Mississippi: Golden Pond

Cast: Paige, Hildi, Laurie, Amy Wynn

Laurie updates a bedroom by painting the walls camel-yellow, building a large headboard of upholstered aqua fabric with a chocolate brown grid overlay, creating a large mirror from smaller mirrored squares, hanging a thrift store chandelier, adding new upholstered thrift store chairs, using aqua and camel-yellow bedding, and building new chocolate brown bookcases. Hildi adds color to a bathroom (a *Trading Spaces* first!) by stapling more than 6,000 silk flowers to the walls, painting the trim and cabinets gold, creating red acrylic cabinet door insets, building a bench upholstered in terry cloth, and sewing draperies and a shower curtain from French floral fabrics.

E28: Mississippi: Winsmere Way

Cast: Paige, Hildi, Laurie, Amy Wynn

Laurie spices up the bedroom of a newly divorced homeowner with cumin yellow paint on the walls, an eggplant-color ceiling, a large upholstered headboard with nailhead trim, a new chaise lounge, a blown-glass light fixture, and two upholstered message boards. Hildi adds drama to a bedroom by covering the walls in red toile fabric, painting the ceiling smoky plum, slipcovering a thrift store sofa with cream fabric, building a new armoire with curved doors, repainting two thrift store lamps, and creating shadow boxes.

E29: San Antonio, TX: Ghostbridge

Cast: Paige, Hildi, Vern, Ty

Hildi gets groovy in a living room by lining one wall with record albums and painting the remaining walls purple, yellow, teal, and orange. She creates slipcovers in the same colors, makes a coffee tabletop by covering a colorful scarf with a large piece of glass, paints the homeowners' favorite chair black with brightly colored flowers, installs lamps made from French drainpipes, and designs a large entertainment center. Vern leaves his mark in a living room by covering one wall with wood veneer wallpaper, bringing in new pieces of brown furniture, hanging red draperies, creating a red and gold leaf coffee table and room screen, and laying a red rug.

E30: Austin, TX: Wyoming Valley Drive

Cast: Paige, Hildi, Laurie, Ty

Laurie adds warmth to a dining room by weaving one wall with brown sueded cotton and painting the other walls pink-orange. She builds a round dining table with a stenciled top and a fabric skirt, designs a buffet table with legs made from plumbing conduit, and makes

Gen's Room
Dusty Trail, California

after ◀

draperies and seat cushions from green fabric. Hildi creates a sleek kitchen by covering the walls with peel-and-stick wine labels, painting the cabinets black, enlarging an existing bench, designing a large pot rack from lumber and copper plumbing conduit, painting the existing wooden blinds black and orange, slipcovering the dining chairs with orange fabric, and embellishing the dining table with gold accents.

E31: Austin, TX: Aire Libre Drive

Cast: Paige, Frank, Kia, Ty

Frank adds drama to a living room by painting one wall orange and the other walls yellow, building two new end tables, designing a massive coffee table out of a black granite slab and four decorative columns, adding a toy chest to hold dog toys, covering the existing furniture with multicolor fabric, and laying a new rug. Kia updates a living room by painting the walls moss green and brown, painting a golden glaze over the brown paint, designing new draperies from various types of printed fabric, building a large frame above the fireplace, adding a new love seat, and scavenging accessories from other rooms in the house.

E32: Austin, TX: Wampton Way

Cast: Paige, Doug, Genevieve, Ty

Gen adds an Art Deco touch to a living room by colorwashing the walls in various shades of yellow and orange, slipcovering the existing furniture with graphic black and white fabric, building up the existing fireplace with black and mahogany accents, suspending the television with cables and a wooden shelf, adding two large topiaries, and framing various champagne and liqueur posters. Doug gives a living room an antique

Spanish flair by building a large dark brown fireplace facade, painting the walls smoky green, and staining the existing barstools a darker brown. He adds a chair upholstered in newspaper-print fabric and creates wall art with canvas and newspapers.

E33: San Clemente, CA: Camino Mojada

Cast: Paige, Genevieve, Vern, Ty

Gen adds Polynesian flair to a bedroom by building a grass-cloth headboard, hanging mosquito netting, painting the walls smoky taupe, painting the existing furniture orange, sewing two new dog beds from the same material as the new bedspread, planting several large palm plants, and building a large square shelving unit to hold accessories and a TV. Vern cozies up a loft TV room by attaching several upholstered diamond shapes on two walls, building new black velvet upholstered sofas, designing a large black coffee table with upholstered panels, framing photocopies of Hollywood movie legends on vellum, installing new shelving to hold entertainment equipment, and hanging several black and taupe drapery panels to close off the room.

E34: California: Dusty Trail

Cast: Paige, Doug, Genevieve, Ty

Doug designs a bedroom he calls "Cosmo Shab" by colorwashing the walls with three shades of blue paint, painting the cathedral ceiling gray, installing crown molding, hanging a chandelier removed from the dining room, sewing gray and white toile draperies, painting the existing furniture white, and distressing the newly painted pieces to create an antique look. Gen transforms a kitchen into a French *boucherie* (butcher shop) by covering the walls with green chalkboard paint, painting the cabinets vanilla with gray insets, installing a tin ceiling, building a larger tabletop, and hanging pictures of "meat puppets" around the room.

E35: California: Fairfield
Cast: Paige, Frank, Kia, Ty
Kia updates an office/game room by painting the walls apricot and the trim orange. She builds a love seat that sits 8 inches off the ground, designs a removable tabletop for an existing game table, builds storage cubes that double as seats, hangs a "mirror" made of CDs, makes chess pieces from copper pipe, and rearranges the existing desk to create a more effective office area. Frank designs a "tranquil love nest" in a bedroom, adding coffee-color paint, a new coffee bar (complete with a small refrigerator), wooden chevrons on the existing furniture, gauzy fabric draped around the four-poster bed, and a large piece of bamboo for a drapery rod.

E36: San Diego, CA: Duenda Road
Cast: Paige, Frank, Vern, Amy Wynn
Frank adds romance to a bedroom by painting the walls soft green, building a canopy frame from molding strips, hanging a gauzy canopy from the ceiling, and revamping an existing dresser. Vern updates a living room by painting the walls with two tones of soft green, surrounding the existing fireplace with slate tiles, painting the existing furniture a third shade of green, hanging glass vases on the wall, installing green chenille draperies, and creating a new entertainment center.

E37: Los Angeles, CA: Murietta Avenue
Cast: Paige, Genevieve, Laurie, Amy Wynn
Gen gives a bland living/dining room a 1940s L.A. twist by painting the walls dark red, painting the trim bright white, adding white crown molding, and hanging draperies featuring a palm frond print. Gen also designs lighted display shelves, frames book illustrations of L.A. in the 1940s, reupholsters the dining room chairs with more palm frond fabrics, and hangs a new period light fixture. Laurie creates a warm and comfortable living room by

painting the walls butter yellow, with bands of golden camel and cream near the top of the walls. She installs built-in wall cabinets to house electronic equipment and "hideaway dog beds," lays a large khaki area rug, paints the fireplace white, slipcovers the sofa, and adds two green chenille chairs.

E38: Scottsdale, AZ: Bell Road
Cast: Paige, Frank, Vern, Ty
Frank adds a touch of whimsy to a girl's bedroom by painting geometric shapes on the walls with different shades of pastel paints; painting different sections of the walls purple; installing a desk unit that looks like a monkey; laying a multicolor rug; designing a doll-inspired TV cabinet; and adding blue beanbag chairs, multicolored linens, and large throw pillows. Vern creates a soothingly sexy bedroom by painting two walls deep purple, covering two walls and the ceiling with maple planks, building a birch platform bed, installing a cable lighting fixture, hanging mirrored candle sconces throughout the room, designing a long entertainment/storage bench, and re-covering an existing sofa with dark purple fabric.

E39: Scottsdale, AZ: Windrose Avenue
Cast: Paige, Doug, Frank, Ty
Doug transforms a large bedroom into two intimate areas by building a large I-shape wall in the center of the room: He places the existing bed on one side of the wall and places a sofa and armoire removed from other rooms in the house on the other side of the wall. He also paints the walls yellow and the new wall rust-red, sews new rust and yellow bedding with mod square embellishments, designs a plank-style coffee table, and hangs two of the homeowners' favorite tulip paintings on each side of the wall. He titles the room "Barrier." Frank transports a bedroom to India during the colonial period by painting the walls deep purple, reusing the existing navy drapes, adding a navy valance with gold stenciling, creating nightstands from inverted bamboo trash cans, adding lamps with beaded shades, and converting an existing dresser into a TV armoire.

E40: Vegas, NV: Carlsbad Caverns
Cast: Paige, Doug, Hildi, Amy Wynn
To redecorate a living room, Hildi draws inspiration from a print she bought in London. She paints the walls dark red; paints the ceiling blue; adds six red columns throughout the room; lays checkerboard vinyl flooring in two shades of orange; hangs deep red draperies; and adds slipcovers, upholstery, and pillows in every shade of the rainbow. Doug gets "Dirty" in a bedroom by covering the walls in dark brown Venetian plaster. He paints the ceiling peach, hangs bright blue draperies, sews pillows and bedding in various blue fabrics, installs crown molding, builds a large round white armoire, and creates a four-poster look around the existing bed with four alleged stripper poles.

E41: Vegas, NV: Smokemont Courts
Cast: Paige, Edward, Laurie, Amy Wynn
Edward designs a hip, funky office with one purple wall. He paints the remaining walls and ceiling light gray, constructs a large black built-in desk, designs black shelving, uses the homeowner's guitars as artwork, creates window shades from plastic sheets and paper clips, drapes white fabric across one wall, and incorporates a gray flannel chaise lounge. Laurie updates a bland living room by painting the walls taupe, building a large square shelving unit, painting the shelving insets coral, laying a large brown area rug, hanging conduit piping as drapery rods, hanging a piece of fabric as artwork, utilizing the existing black love seats, adding a square coffee table, and converting an existing side table into an ottoman.

E42: Vegas, NV: Woodmore Court
Cast: Paige, Genevieve, Vern, Amy Wynn
Gen goes bold in a living room by painting plant ledges in various shades of purple, building a dark wooden surround for the fireplace and TV cabinet, hanging two raspberry-shape light fixtures, painting a stained-glass treatment on the windows, designing a square coffee table with an inset basket center filled with floating candles, and hanging long white linen curtains. Vern re-creates the feel of a breezy summer day in a living room by painting light yellow 1-foot-wide stripes across the walls, building a large white armoire, adding doors that match the armoire to an existing wall niche, slipcovering the existing furniture with blue fabric, transforming two thrift store computer desks into a square coffee table, and installing white crown molding.

E43: Miami, FL: Ten Court
Cast: Paige, Hildi, Kia, Ty
Hildi adds an art gallery look to a living room with periwinkle blue walls, a slipcovered thrift store sofa to match the walls, a new brick paver floor, a wooden slat bench-style coffee table, track lighting, and canvases covered in several pastel paints blended into one another. Kia heads toward

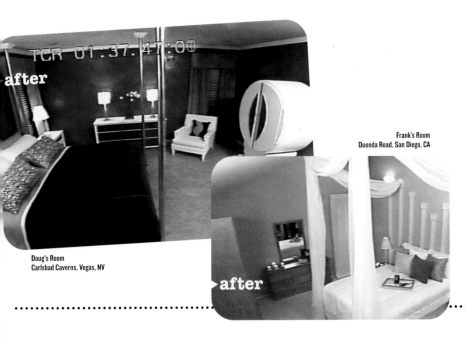

after

Doug's Room
Carlsbad Caverns, Vegas, NV

Frank's Room
Duenda Road, San Diego, CA

after

the sea in a bedroom with shell-shape head- and footboards, sea blue walls, bedside shelves made from bamboo, window shades made with fabric stretched across a bamboo frame, a wide wallpaper border, and a sea-grass rug.

E44: Miami, FL: Miami Place

Cast: Paige, Hildi, Laurie, Ty

Hildi sees spots in a large living room by upholstering several pieces of furniture with cream fabric covered in white and black circles, painting the walls to match the fabric, building a circular shelving unit/entertainment center, repairing existing water damage on the walls, hanging matchstick blinds, and laying a new khaki carpet. Laurie warms a bland living room with gold paint and by creating a molding design on the ceiling, hanging a square light fixture, constructing a large built-in cabinet for the big-screen TV, creating a seating area and a dining area, and designing a Hans Hofmann-inspired painting for the new dining area.

E45: Miramar, FL: Avenue 164

Cast: Paige, Doug, Frank, Ty

Doug energizes a bland white kitchen by painting the walls citron green and the cabinets tomato red, adding concentric rectangles to the cabinet fronts with molding, replacing some drawers with dark brown wicker baskets, and adding several brightly colored plants in white pots throughout the room. Paige names Doug's room "Contemporibbean Kitchen." Frank looks to the future in a bedroom by painting the walls deep red, building a headboard out of various upholstered shapes, sewing a duvet cover from vintage fabric, painting the existing furniture black, hanging long black doors around the room as artwork, and designing a large black futuristically styled entertainment center.

Laurie's Room
Ocean Park, Santa Monica, CA

E46: Orlando, FL: Smith Street

Cast: Paige, Hildi, Kia, Amy Wynn

Hildi helps reorganize the space in an efficiency apartment by painting the walls yellow, building a large bed unit that can be used as a king-size bed or divided so the homeowner's daughter has her own space when she visits, making a roll screen from her own photo of the Arc d'Triumph to divide the bed, adding a dining/entertaining area with thrift store tables and chairs, reconfiguring the closet storage to include a desk area, and painting the carpet brown. Kia remakes a bedroom in a Moroccan theme, painting the walls green, hanging purple, green, and gold draperies; adding a copper glaze to the ceiling; installing a ceiling fan; building a large headboard with a Moroccan-motif cutout; hanging wallpaper "columns" on the wall; and replacing the existing closet doors with mirrored ones.

E47: Florida: Night Owl Lane

Cast: Paige, Edward, Hildi, Amy Wynn

Edward adds Eastern flair to a bedroom by painting the walls yellow; designing a headboard with decoratively framed bulletin boards and a footboard with stylized feet; installing two bedside tables mounted to the wall; painting a piece of custom artwork of a Buddha image; antiquing a thrift store dresser, mirror, and bench; hanging brown fabric on the windows; and hanging white curtains stenciled with brown henna-style markings to disguise the dressing area. Hildi streamlines a large art collection by building a new wall with several large shelves to display paintings, texturing the walls with stucco, laying a parquet floor, and changing the furniture configuration.

E48: Los Angeles, CA: Elm Street (Celebrity Episode)

Cast: Paige, Genevieve, Vern, Ty

Gen updates Sarah Rue's office by painting the walls smoky taupe and the trim brown, building a mahogany L-shape corner desk out of two doors and two oxidized filing cabinets, designing a banquette/lounge seating area, adding red decorative accents, and displaying framed line drawings of cats created by her team. Vern adds warmth to Andy Dick's kitchen and breakfast nook by painting the walls two different shades of terra-cotta, installing a faux-terra-cotta tile floor and a brown tile countertop, adding wrought-iron hardware and decorative accents, painting a graphic circular image across several canvases, and sewing rust-tone Roman shades.

E49: Santa Monica, CA: Ocean Park

Cast: Paige, Laurie, Vern, Ty

Laurie unifies a living room by painting the walls yellow, adding a ready-made desk, hanging Gottlieb-inspired paintings on either side of the fireplace, building out the existing fireplace with a new mantel, laying a new area rug, installing wall shelves, and adding horseshoe-shape

chairs. Vern designs a meditative look in a bedroom by painting the walls light blue, building a large white headboard with a square inset shelf to hold a Buddha statue, installing a large entertainment center/shelving unit, adding two bedside tables, and hanging a silver-leaf candle shelf.

E50: Los Angeles, CA: Irving Street

Cast: Paige, Frank, Genevieve, Ty

Frank adds a modern twist to a bachelor's living room by painting the walls sky blue, adding black and taupe paint to the fireplace, buying all new furniture and lamps, building a wood bar, framing a black and white string art project, and hanging several of the homeowner's photos. Gen looks to orchids for color inspiration in a living room and paints the walls white and the trim green, installs green molding on the curved ceiling, builds a low-slung sofa and a new dining table, and hangs three line drawings of orchids.

E51: California: Via Jardin

Cast: Paige, Laurie, Vern, Amy Wynn

Laurie warms up a living room by painting the walls orange, painting large bookshelves with black and red lacquer, building a vertical fireplace extension with an octagon motif made from decorative molding, creating a bamboo-framed full-length mirror, slipcovering the furniture with white fabric, and accenting a long wall with a row of white vertical rectangles made from molding. Vern softens the colors in a kitchen by painting the "slaughterhouse red" walls yellow-cream, expanding the island top, designing a seating bench with inside storage, turning a tall bookcase on its side to become a bench/shoe storage area, hanging stainless-steel pot shelving above the stove, and laying new wood laminate flooring.

E52: Los Angeles, CA: Seventh Street (Celebrity Episode)

Cast: Paige, Edward, Hildi, Amy Wynn

Edward gets funky in Beverly Mitchell's garage rec room by painting the walls gray; building room screens that are painted gray and chartreuse; upholstering thrift store and existing furniture with chartreuse fabric; building a bar area; hanging white, gray, and chartreuse curtains on rods made of bent pipe to hide the laundry area; and hanging paper lanterns over the seating area. Hildi brings a little refinement to George and Jeff Stoltz's bachelor pad living room by covering the walls with blue faux suede, laying a khaki carpet, building a large armoire with woven raffia doors, installing a small wall near the front door to create a short hallway, reupholstering two thrift store sofas, building a small bar-style table, hanging a bike spray-painted silver on the wall as sculpture, and framing black and white photos of Hildi's and her team's tummies.

E53: Orlando, FL: Winter Song Drive

Cast: Paige, Doug, Vern, Ty

Doug gives an enclosed patio a martini bar look by painting

>after

Doug's Room
Winter Song Drive, Orlando, FL

the walls white, adding a marble tile top to an existing bar, covering the front of the bar with aluminum flashing, mounting a TV on the wall, hanging multiple white waterproof curtains, using silver conduit as a drapery rod, building banquette and upholstered cube seating, and attaching several round automotive mirrors to the wall. Vern gives new life to a living room by painting three walls taupe and one wall rust-red, laying a new sea-grass rug, painting the existing armoire tan and the side tables rust-red, building an upholstered removable top for the coffee table so it can double as an ottoman, and buying a brown sectional sofa from a thrift store.

E54: Orlando, FL: Whisper Lake
Cast: Paige, Frank, Hildi, Amy Wynn
Frank lightens a family room by dry-brushing the walls with white paint and the wainscoting with sage green paint, adding a broken tile mosaic to the existing fireplace, hanging fishnetting as a valance, upholstering the existing furniture with sage green fabric, painting the existing armoire pale blue, and installing lighthouse-themed hardware on the armoire doors and drawers. Hildi spices up a living room by painting the walls red, upholstering the furniture in and making draperies from cream fabric printed with red Asian-themed designs, building a new wall to better define the space, demolishing a small half-wall, transforming wicker chicken cages into light fixtures, and painting the coffee and side tables black.

E55: South Carolina: Innisbrook Lane
Cast: Paige, Frank, Laurie, Carter
Frank brightens a large living room by painting the walls yellow, decoupaging green and white marbled paper to insets on the fireplace, hanging navy blue drapes, slipcovering the furniture in both red and taupe fabric, laying a large natural-tone rug, and covering the bases of two new lamps with the same paper used on the fireplace. Laurie revamps a living room with a color

palette inspired by a van Gogh print. Three walls are painted sage green; the remaining wall is painted with horizontal stripes in sage green, olive green, yellow, and white; a new silver light fixture is hung; the furniture is rearranged into a more comfortable conversation area; doors are added to the existing armoire; and a large square fabric-topped coffee table is built complete with four large storage drawers.

E56: South Carolina: Sherborne Drive
Cast: Paige, Doug, Edward, Carter
Doug creates a comfortable modern den by painting the walls dark plum-gray, laying a dark gray carpet, covering the ceiling with draped sheets of white poster board, installing a long L-shape banquette seating area with circular supports, building upholstered stools, hanging canvases and adding tufted pillows in light lavender shades, and creating a half-wall with strips of wood woven through pipe supports. Edward adds a modern twist to Moroccan style in a living room by painting the ceiling teal, texturing two of the walls with crumpled tissue paper, painting the walls mustard yellow, covering the brick fireplace with terra-cotta-tinted cement, building a large mantel spray-painted to look like stone, and adding wrought-iron decorative accents.

E57: Pennsylvania: Tremont Drive
Cast: Paige, Genevieve, Vern, Amy Wynn
Gen kick-starts a boy's bedroom by painting the walls bright green, adding a black and white racing stripe around the room on the center of the walls, building a raised platform for the bed and desk, creating a seating area with a green rug and orange chairs, suspending several green and white paper lanterns above the bed, and adding multiple pieces of hockey memorabilia around the room. Vern designs an inviting living room by painting the walls gold, applying copper leaf to a large inset in the ceiling, slipcovering an existing and a thrift

store sofa in brown velvet, building a chaise lounge, tiling the top of the existing coffee table with brown and gold glass tiles, and creating a large burgundy cabinet/bar wall unit by mixing ready-made and newly constructed pieces.

E58: Pennsylvania: Bryant Court
Cast: Paige, Hildi, Laurie, Amy Wynn
Hildi makes a bold statement in a dining room by painting the walls and ceiling black, painting a thrift store table and chairs bright golden yellow, installing a large black light fixture that holds 53 exposed lightbulbs, hanging cream draperies, upholstering the dining chairs with twig-print cream fabric, hanging metal screens spray-painted chrome on the wall, and creating several flower arrangements in vases filled with boiled eggs. Laurie pumps up the pizzazz in a room shared by two little girls by painting the walls bright green, hand painting large pink and yellow zinnias across the walls, building square headboards upholstered in pink and yellow plaid fabric, creating two new toy boxes painted with each girl's initials, painting the existing furniture and trim yellow, and creating a small tea table area. She names the room "Zany for Zinnias."

E59: Pennsylvania: Cresheim Road
Cast: Paige, Hildi, Kia, Amy Wynn
Hildi goes glam in an office by painting the walls and trim magenta, laying black foam squares as carpeting, building an 11-foot-long couch upholstered in pink python-print vinyl with white lights underneath, sewing purple sequined throw pillows, hanging magenta velvet drapes, installing a large white desk unit, and adding a magenta chair. She names the room "Mom's Lipstick Palace." Kia gets musical in a kitchen by painting the walls "turmeric yellow," painting the trim white, installing a sheet-metal backsplash, adding new cabinets and countertops, decoupaging sheet music on the top of a new island, suspending a trombone to be used as a pot rack, installing a ceiling fan, and creating a cabinet door that looks like a large bass complete with vintage accessories.

>after

Hildi's Room
Whisper Lake, Orlando, FL

decorating idea index

The following lists give you all the information you need to pinpoint the *Trading Spaces* episodes that feature the room types, styles, themes, and projects you need to inspire your next room makeover.

Each listing includes the episode name, the season and episode number, and the room's designer. Dive in!

Room Types

Basement/Recreational Rooms

Washington, D.C.: Cleveland Park (SI, E7), Doug
Philadelphia, PA: Galahad Road (SI, E12), Gen
Knoxville, TN: Courtney Oak (SI, E13), Frank
Knoxville, TN: Stubbs Bluff (SI, E20), Frank
Quakertown, PA: Quakers Way (S2, E1), Hildi
New Jersey: Tall Pines Drive (S2, E2), Laurie
Philadelphia, PA: Jeannes Street (S2, E10), Gen
Chicago, IL: Fairview Avenue (S2, E16), Gen
Seattle, WA: 56th Place (S2, E23), Hildi
New York: Half Hollow Turn (S3, E7), Kia
Los Angeles, CA: Seventh Street (S3, E52), Edward

Bathrooms

Mississippi: Golden Pond (S3, E27), Hildi

Bedrooms (Adult)

Knoxville, TN: Forest Glen (SI, E2), Doug
Knoxville, TN: Courtney Oak (SI, E13), Laurie
Cincinnati, OH: Madison & Forest (SI, E16), Laurie
San Diego, CA: Elm Ridge (SI, E17), Gen
San Diego, CA: Elm Ridge (SI, E17), Hildi
Miami, FL: 168th/83rd Streets (SI, E21), Dez
Orlando, FL: Lake Catherine (SI, E27), Hildi
Orlando, FL: Gotha Furlong (SI, E28), Gen
Orlando, FL: Gotha Furlong (SI, E28), Frank
New Orleans, LA: Walter Road (SI, E33), Gen
New York: Sherwood Drive (SI, E36), Vern
New York: Sherwood Drive (SI, E36), Doug
New Jersey: Sam Street (SI, E38), Hildi
New Jersey: Tall Pines Drive (S2, E2), Vern
Maple Glen, PA: Fiedler Road (S2, E3), Laurie
Providence, RI: Wallis Avenue (S2, E6), Gen
Boston, MA: Institute Road (S2, E9), Doug
New Jersey: Perth Road (S2, E11), Laurie
Maryland: Village Green (S2, E12), Gen
Maryland: Village Green (S2, E12), Doug

Maryland: Fairway Court (S2, E13), Vern
Maryland: Fairway Court (S2, E13), Doug
Chicago, IL: Spaulding Avenue (S2, E15), Hildi
Colorado: Stoneflower Drive (S2, E20), Frank
Seattle, WA: Dakota Street (S2, E22), Laurie
Oregon: Alyssum Avenue (S2, E24), Hildi
California: Corte Rosa (S2, E28), Vern
California: Corte Rosa (S2, E28), Laurie
California: Grenadine Way (S2, E29), Vern
Austin, TX: La Costa Drive (S2, E36), Vern
Texas: Sherwood Street (S2, E37), Gen
Houston, TX: Appalachian Trail (S2, E39), Doug
Plano, TX: Shady Valley Road (S2, E41), Hildi
Raleigh, NC: Legging Lane (S2, E43), Hildi
North Carolina: Southerby Drive (S2, E44), Doug
North Carolina: Southerby Drive (S2, E44), Hildi
Wake Forest, NC: Rodney Bay (S2, E45), Vern
Maine: Joseph Drive (S3, E3), Laurie
Maine: Joseph Drive (S3, E3), Frank
Long Island, NY: Steuben Boulevard (S3, E4), Edward
New York: Whitlock Road (S3, E6), Gen
New York: Whitlock Road (S3, E6), Doug
Philadelphia, PA: 22nd Street (S3, E8), Gen
Pennsylvania: Gorski Lane (S3, E10), Frank
Pennsylvania: Gorski Lane (S3, E10), Doug
Long Island, NY: Dover Court (S3, E11), Edward
Pennsylvania: Victoria Drive (S3, E12), Kia
New Jersey: Catania Court (S3, E15), Hildi
Virginia: Gentle Heights Court (S3, E17), Kia
Arlington, VA: First Road (S3, E18), Hildi
Arlington, VA: First Road (S3, E18), Doug
Washington, D.C.: Quebec Place (S3, E19), Vern
Indiana: Fieldhurst Lane (S3, E21), Doug
Indiana: Fieldhurst Lane (S3, E21), Vern
Indianapolis, IN: Halleck Way (S3, E22), Edward
Indianapolis, IN: Halleck Way (S3, E22), Kia
Missouri: Sunburst Drive (S3, E23), Gen
Missouri: Sunburst Drive (S3, E23), Vern
Missouri: Sweetbriar Lane (S3, E25), Edward
Missouri: Sweetbriar Lane (S3, E25), Frank
London, England: Garden Flat (S3, E26), Gen
Mississippi: Golden Pond (S3, E27), Laurie
Mississippi: Winsmere Way (S3, E28), Laurie

Mississippi: Winsmere Way (S3, E28), Hildi
San Clemente, CA: Camino Mojada (S3, E33), Gen
California: Dusty Trail (S3, E34), Doug
California: Fairfield (S3, E35), Frank
San Diego, CA: Duenda Road (S3, E36), Frank
Scottsdale, AZ: Bell Road (S3, E38), Vern
Scottsdale, AZ: Windrose Avenue (S3, E39), Doug
Scottsdale, AZ: Windrose Avenue (S3, E39), Frank
Vegas, NV: Carlsbad Caverns (S3, E40), Doug
Miami, FL: Ten Court (S3, E43), Kia
Miramar, FL: Avenue 164 (S3, E45), Frank
Orlando, FL: Smith Street (S3, E46), Kia
Florida: Night Owl Lane (S3, E47), Edward
Santa Monica, CA: Ocean Park (S3, E49), Vern

Bedrooms (Children's)

Athens, GA: County Road (SI, E3), Frank
Cincinnati, OH: Sturbridge Road (SI, E15), Gen
Orlando, FL: Winterhaven (SI, E29), Doug
New Orleans, LA: D'evereaux Street (SI, E34), Vern
Boston, MA: Ashfield Street (S2, E7), Laurie
Boston, MA: Ashfield Street (S2, E7), Gen
Long Island, NY: Dover Court (S3, E11), Vern
Virginia: Gentle Heights Court (S3, E17), Hildi
Scott Air Force Base, MO: Ash Creek (S3, E24), Doug
London, England: Garden Flat (S3, E26), Hildi
Scottsdale, AZ: Bell Road (S3, E38), Frank
Pennsylvania: Tremont Drive (S3, E57), Gen
Pennsylvania: Bryant Court (S3, E58), Laurie

Dens

Knoxville, TN: Fourth & Gill (SI, E1), Frank
Boston, MA: Institute Road (S2, E9), Frank
South Carolina: Sherborne Drive (S3, E56), Doug

Dining Rooms

Alpharetta, GA: Providence Oaks (SI, E4), Hildi
Philadelphia, PA: Valley Road (SI, E11), Laurie
Cincinnati, OH: Sturbridge Road (SI, E15), Doug
Austin, TX: Wycliff (SI, E24), Hildi
New Jersey: Sam Street (SI, E38), Laurie
California: Peralta Street (S2, E32), Doug
Los Angeles, CA: Springdale Drive (S2, E34), Vern
Long Island, NY: Steuben Boulevard (S3, E4), Frank
New Jersey: Catania Court (S3, E15), Gen
Austin, TX: Wyoming Valley Drive (S3, E30), Laurie
Pennsylvania: Bryant Court (S3, E58), Hildi

Family Rooms

Portland, OR: Everett Street (S2, E26), Doug
Orlando, FL: Whisper Lake (S3, E54), Frank

Kitchens

Knoxville, TN: Fourth & Gill (SI, E1), Laurie
Buckhead, GA: Canter Road (SI, E6), Gen
Alexandria, VA: Riefton Court (SI, E8), Frank
Annapolis, MD: Fox Hollow (SI, E9), Laurie

Cincinnati, OH: Melrose Avenue (SI, EI4), Hildi
San Diego, CA: Hermes Avenue (SI, EI8), Laurie
San Diego, CA: Wilbur Street (SI, EI9), Doug
Knoxville, TN: Stubbs Bluff (SI, E20), Doug
Fort Lauderdale, FL: 59th Street (SI, E22), Hildi
Austin, TX: Wycliff (SI, E24), Doug
Austin, TX: Wing Road (SI, E25), Gen
Orlando, FL: Lake Catherine (SI, E27), Vern
Santa Fe, NM: Felize (SI, E3I), Vern
New Orleans, LA: Jacob Street (SI, E32), Hildi
New Orleans, LA: Walter Road (SI, E33), Frank
New Jersey: Lincroft (SI, E39), Laurie
Providence, RI: Wallis Avenue (S2, E6), Frank
Chicago, IL: Edward Road (S2, EI4), Frank
Chicago, IL: Fairview Avenue (S2, EI6), Vern
Colorado: Berry Avenue (S2, EI7), Gen
Oregon: Alsea Court (S2, E25), Frank
Oakland, CA: Webster Street (S2, E3I), Gen
Texas: Sherwood Street (S2, E37), Frank
Texas: Sutton Court (S2, E42), Laurie
Maine: George Road (S3, EI), Doug
Maine: George Road (S3, EI), Gen
Long Island, NY: Split Rock Road (S3, E5), Gen
Long Island, NY: Split Rock Road (S3, E5), Vern
Philadelphia, PA: Gettysburg Lane (S3, E9), Frank
Nazareth, PA: First Street (S3, EI4), Doug
Austin, TX: Wyoming Valley Drive (S3, E30), Hildi
California: Dusty Trail (S3, E34), Gen
Miramar, FL: Avenue I64 (S3, E45), Doug
California: Via Jardin (S3, E5I), Vern
Pennsylvania: Cresheim Road (S3, E59), Kia

Living Rooms

Knoxville, TN: Forest Glen (SI, E2), Hildi
Lawrenceville, GA: Pine Lane (SI, E5), Dez
Lawrenceville, GA: Pine Lane (SI, E5), Hildi
Buckhead, GA: Canter Road (SI, E6), Laurie
Washington, D.C.: Cleveland Park (SI, E7), Dez
Alexandria, VA: Riefton Court (SI, E8), Gen
Annapolis, MD: Fox Hollow (SI, E9), Gen
Philadelphia, PA: Strathmore Road (SI, EIO), Frank
Philadelphia, PA: Strathmore Road (SI, EIO), Dez
Cincinnati, OH: Melrose Avenue (SI, EI4), Frank
Cincinnati, OH: Madison & Forest (SI, EI6), Doug
San Diego, CA: Hermes Avenue (SI, EI8), Gen
San Diego, CA: Wilbur Street (SI, EI9), Frank
Miami, FL: I68th/83rd Streets (SI, E2I), Laurie
Fort Lauderdale, FL: 59th Street (SI, E22), Frank
Key West, FL: Elizabeth Street (SI, E23), Frank
Key West, FL: Elizabeth Street (SI, E23), Gen
Austin, TX: Wing Road (SI, E25), Hildi
Austin, TX: Birdhouse Drive (SI, E26), Frank
Orlando, FL: Winterhaven (SI, E29), Laurie
Albuquerque, NM: Gloria (SI, E30), Hildi
Albuquerque, NM: Gloria (SI, E30), Doug
Santa Fe, NM: Felize (SI, E3I), Gen
New York: Shore Road (SI, E35), Dez

New York: Linda Court (SI, E37), Doug
New York: Linda Court (SI, E37), Frank
New Jersey: Lincroft (SI, E39), Doug
New Jersey: Lafayette Street (SI, E40), Vern
Quakertown, PA: Quakers Way (S2, EI), Doug
Maple Glen, PA: Fiedler Road (S2, E3), Gen
Northampton, PA: James Avenue (S2, E4), Hildi
Northampton, PA: James Avenue (S2, E4), Frank
Providence, RI: Phillips Street (S2, E5), Hildi
Providence, RI: Phillips Street (S2, E5), Vern
Springfield, MA: Sunset Terrace (S2, E8), Hildi
Springfield, MA: Sunset Terrace (S2, E8), Vern
Philadelphia, PA: Jeannes Street (S2, EIO), Vern
New Jersey: Perth Road (S2, EII), Frank
Chicago, IL: Edward Road (S2, EI4), Laurie
Chicago, IL: Spaulding Avenue (S2, EI5), Doug
Colorado: Berry Avenue (S2, EI7), Hildi
Colorado: Cherry Street (S2, EI8), Gen
Colorado: Cherry Street (S2, EI8), Laurie
Colorado: Andes Way (S2, EI9), Frank
Colorado: Andes Way (S2, EI9), Vern
Colorado: Stoneflower Drive (S2, E20), Doug
Seattle, WA: I37th Street (S2, E2I), Doug
Seattle, WA: I37th Street (S2, E2I), Frank
Seattle, WA: Dakota Street (S2, E22), Vern
Seattle, WA: 56th Place (S2, E23), Gen
Oregon: Alyssum Avenue (S2, E24), Gen
Oregon: Alsea Court (S2, E25), Laurie
Santa Clara, CA: Lafayette Street (S2, E27), Frank
California: Grenadine Way (S2, E29), Frank
Oakland, CA: Webster Street (S2, E3I), Hildi
California: Peralta Street (S2, E32), Hildi
Los Angeles, CA: Willoughby Avenue (S2, E33), Doug
Los Angeles, CA: Willoughby Avenue (S2, E33), Gen
California: Abbeywood Lane (S2, E35), Frank
California: Abbeywood Lane (S2, E35), Hildi
Houston, TX: Sawdust Street (S2, E38), Laurie
Houston, TX: Sawdust Street (S2, E38), Doug
Plano, TX: Bent Horn Court (S2, E40), Vern
Texas: Sutton Court (S2, E42), Frank
Wake Forest, NC: Rodney Bay (S2, E45), Laurie
Portland, OR: Rosemont Avenue (S3, E2), Laurie
Portland, OR: Rosemont Avenue (S3, E2), Vern
New York: Half Hollow Turn (S3, E7), Frank
Philadelphia, PA: 22nd Street (S3, E8), Edward
Philadelphia, PA: Gettysburg Lane (S3, E9), Vern
Pennsylvania: Victoria Drive (S3, EI2), Doug
New Jersey: Manitoba Trail (S3, EI3), Doug
Nazareth, PA: First Street (S3, EI4), Vern
Philadelphia, PA: East Avenue (S3, EI6), Hildi
Philadelphia, PA: East Avenue (S3, EI6), Frank
Washington, D.C.: Quebec Place (S3, EI9), Gen
Indianapolis, IN: River Valley Drive (S3, E20), Gen
Indianapolis, IN: River Valley Drive (S3, E20), Doug
San Antonio, TX: Ghostbridge (S3, E29), Hildi
San Antonio, TX: Ghostbridge (S3, E29), Vern
Austin, TX: Aire Libre Drive (S3, E3I), Frank

Austin, TX: Aire Libre Drive (S3, E3I), Kia
Austin, TX: Wampton Way (S3, E32), Gen
Austin, TX: Wampton Way (S3, E32), Doug
San Diego, CA: Duenda Road (S3, E36), Vern
Los Angeles, CA: Murietta Avenue (S3, E37), Laurie
Vegas, NV: Carlsbad Caverns (S3, E40), Hildi
Vegas, NV: Smokemont Courts (S3, E4I), Laurie
Vegas, NV: Woodmore Court (S3, E42), Gen
Vegas, NV: Woodmore Court (S3, E42), Vern
Miami, FL: Ten Court (S3, E43), Hildi
Miami, FL: Miami Place (S3, E44), Hildi
Miami, FL: Miami Place (S3, E44), Laurie
Florida: Night Owl Lane (S3, E47), Hildi
Santa Monica, CA: Ocean Park (S3, E49), Laurie
Los Angeles, CA: Irving Street (S3, E50), Frank
Los Angeles, CA: Irving Street (S3, E50), Gen
California: Via Jardin (S3, E5I), Laurie
Los Angeles, CA: Seventh Street (S3, E52), Hildi
Orlando, FL: Winter Song Drive (S3, E53), Vern
Orlando, FL: Whisper Lake (S3, E54), Hildi
South Carolina: Innisbrook Lane (S3, E55), Frank
South Carolina: Innisbrook Lane (S3, E55), Laurie
South Carolina: Sherborne Drive (S3, E56), Edward
Pennsylvania: Tremont Drive (S3, E57), Vern

Multipurpose Rooms

Athens, GA: County Road (SI, E3), Hildi
   (kitchen/living room)
Alpharetta, GA: Providence Oaks (SI, E4),
   Roderick (den/guest room)
Philadelphia, PA: Galahad Road (SI, EI2), Hildi
   (living/dining room)
Austin, TX: Birdhouse Drive (SI, E26), Laurie
   (living/dining room)
New Orleans, LA: Jacob Street (SI, E32), Laurie
   (kitchen/office/dining/living room)
New Orleans, LA: D'evereaux Street (SI, E34),
   Gen (den/guest room)
New Jersey: Lafayette Street (SI, E40), Frank
   (dining/living room)
Portland, OR: Everett Street (S2, E26), Vern
   (living/dining room)
Houston, TX: Appalachian Trail (S2, E39), Laurie
   (office/playroom)
New Jersey: Manitoba Trail (S3, EI3), Frank
   (living/dining room)
Scott Air Force Base, MO: Ash Creek (S3, E24),
   Kia (living/dining room)
California: Fairfield (S3, E35), Kia (office/game
   room)
Los Angeles, CA: Murietta Avenue (S3, E37), Gen
   (living/dining room)
Orlando, FL: Smith Street (S3, E46), Hildi
   (bedroom/dining room/entertaining
   area/office)
Los Angeles, CA: Elm Street (S3, E48), Vern
   (kitchen/breakfast nook)

New Jersey: Manitoba Trail (S3, E13), Frank
New Jersey: Catania Court (S3, E15), Hildi
Austin, TX: Aire Libre Drive (S3, E31), Kia
Austin, TX: Wampton Way (S3, E32), Doug
California: Dusty Trail (S3, E34), Gen
San Diego, CA: Duenda Road (S3, E36), Frank
San Diego, CA: Duenda Road (S3, E36), Vern
Miramar, FL: Avenue 164 (S3, E45), Doug
Orlando, FL: Smith Street (S3, E46), Kia
South Carolina: Innisbrook Lane (S3, E55), Laurie
Pennsylvania: Tremont Drive (S3, E57), Gen
Pennsylvania: Bryant Court (S3, E58), Laurie

Blues

Philadelphia, PA: Valley Road (S1, E11), Doug
Knoxville, TN: Courtney Oak (S1, E13), Frank
San Diego, CA: Hermes Avenue (S1, E18), Laurie
Key West, FL: Elizabeth Street (S1, E23), Frank
Santa Fe, NM: Felize (S1, E31), Vern
New York: Sherwood Drive (S1, E36), Vern
Quakertown, PA: Quakers Way (S2, E1), Hildi
Providence, RI: Wallis Avenue (S2, E6), Frank
Boston, MA: Ashfield Street (S2, E7), Gen
Maryland: Fairway Court (S2, E13), Doug
Oregon: Alyssum Avenue (S2, E24), Hildi
California: Grenadine Way (S2, E29), Vern
Los Angeles, CA: Willoughby Avenue (S2, E33), Gen
Houston, TX: Appalachian Trail (S2, E39), Doug
North Carolina: Southerby Drive (S2, E44), Doug
Portland, OR: Rosemont Avenue (S3, E2), Laurie
Long Island, NY: Dover Court (S3, E11), Vern
Virginia: Gentle Heights Court (S3, E17), Hildi
Arlington, VA: First Road (S3, E18), Hildi
Indiana: Fieldhurst Lane (S3, E21), Vern
Missouri: Sunburst Drive (S3, E23), Vern
California: Dusty Trail (S3, E34), Doug
Miami, FL: Ten Court (S3, E43), Hildi
Miami, FL: Ten Court (S3, E43), Kia
Santa Monica, CA: Ocean Park (S3, E49), Vern
Los Angeles, CA: Irving Street (S3, E50), Frank
Los Angeles, CA: Seventh Street (S3, E52), Hildi

Purples

Athens, GA: County Road (S1, E3), Frank
Alpharetta, GA: Providence Oaks (S1, E4), Hildi
Cincinnati, OH: Madison & Forest (S1, E16), Doug
Boston, MA: Ashfield Street (S2, E7), Laurie
Colorado: Berry Avenue (S2, E17), Gen
California: Peralta Street (S2, E32), Hildi
Raleigh, NC: Legging Lane (S2, E43), Hildi
Philadelphia, PA: East Avenue (S3, E16), Frank
Scottsdale, AZ: Bell Road (S3, E38), Frank
Scottsdale, AZ: Bell Road (S3, E38), Vern
Scottsdale, AZ: Windrose Avenue (S3, E39), Frank

Browns

Knoxville, TN: Fourth & Gill (S1, E1), Frank

Buckhead, GA: Canter Road (S1, E6), Laurie
Philadelphia, PA: Strathmore Road (S1, E10), Frank
Philadelphia, PA: Valley Road (S1, E11), Laurie
Philadelphia, PA: Galahad Road (S1, E12), Hildi
Cincinnati, OH: Melrose Avenue (S1, E14), Frank
Cincinnati, OH: Sturbridge Road (S1, E15), Doug
Knoxville, TN: Stubbs Bluff (S1, E20), Frank
Knoxville, TN: Stubbs Bluff (S1, E20), Doug
Austin, TX: Wycliff (S1, E24), Hildi
Santa Fe, NM: Felize (S1, E31), Gen
New York: Sherwood Drive (S1, E36), Doug
New Jersey: Lincroft (S1, E39), Doug
New Jersey: Tall Pines Drive (S2, E2), Vern
Boston, MA: Institute Road (S2, E9), Doug
Maryland: Village Green (S2, E12), Gen
Chicago, IL: Fairview Avenue (S2, E16), Gen
Colorado: Berry Avenue (S2, E17), Hildi
Seattle, WA: 137th Street (S2, E21), Doug
Portland, OR: Everett Street (S2, E26), Doug
Maine: George Road (S3, E1), Doug
New York: Whitlock Road (S3, E6), Gen
Pennsylvania: Victoria Drive (S3, E12), Doug
Indianapolis, IN: Halleck Way (S3, E22), Edward
Missouri: Sunburst Drive (S3, E23), Gen
Vegas, NV: Carlsbad Caverns (S3, E40), Doug
Vegas, NV: Smokemont Courts (S3, E41), Laurie

Taupes/Light Khakis

Alpharetta, GA: Providence Oaks (S1, E4), Roderick
Austin, TX: Wycliff (S1, E24), Doug
Orlando, FL: Gotha Furlong (S1, E28), Frank
New Orleans, LA: Walter Road (S1, E33), Frank
Maple Glen, PA: Fiedler Road (S2, E3) Gen
Springfield, MA: Sunset Terrace (S2, E8), Hildi
New Jersey: Perth Road (S2, E11), Frank
Colorado: Andes Way (S2, E19), Frank
Colorado: Andes Way (S2, E19), Vern
California: Corte Rosa (S2, E28), Vern
Texas: Sutton Court (S3, E42), Laurie
Long Island, NY: Steuben Boulevard (S3, E4), Edward
Nazareth, PA: First Street (S3, E14), Vern
Washington, D.C.: Quebec Place (S3, E19), Gen
San Clemente, CA: Camino Mojada (S3, E33), Gen
San Clemente, CA: Camino Mojada (S3, E33), Vern
California: Fairfield (S3, E35), Frank
Orlando, FL: Winter Song Drive (S3, E53), Vern

Blacks

San Diego, CA: Elm Ridge (S1, E17), Hildi
New Orleans, LA: D'evereaux Street (S1, E34), Vern
Austin, TX: Wyoming Valley Drive (S3, E30), Hildi
Pennsylvania: Bryant Court (S3, E58), Hildi

Grays

Knoxville, TN: Forest Glen (S1, E2), Hildi
Philadelphia, PA: Strathmore Road (S1, E10), Dez
Orlando, FL: Lake Catherine (S1, E27), Hildi

Albuquerque, NM: Gloria (S1, E30), Doug
Providence, RI: Phillips Street (S2, E5), Hildi
Maryland: Village Green (S2, E12), Doug
Maryland: Fairway Court (S2, E13), Vern
Berkeley, CA: Prospect Street (S2, E30), Gen
Wake Forest, NC: Rodney Bay (S2, E45), Vern
Arlington, VA: First Road (S3, E18), Doug
Indiana: River Valley Drive (S3, E20), Gen
Scott Air Force Base, MO: Ash Creek (S3, E24), Doug
Scott Air Force Base, MO: Ash Creek (S3, E24), Kia
Missouri: Sweetbriar Lane (S3, E25), Edward
Vegas, NV: Smokemont Courts (S3, E41), Edward
Los Angeles, CA: Elm Street (S3, E48), Gen
Los Angeles, CA: Seventh Street (S3, E52), Edward
South Carolina: Sherborne Drive (S3, E56), Doug

Whites & Off-Whites

Athens, GA: County Road (S1, E3), Hildi
Lawrenceville, GA: Pine Lane (S1, E5), Dez
Lawrenceville, GA: Pine Lane (S1, E5), Hildi
Fort Lauderdale, FL: 59th Street (S1, E22), Hildi
New Orleans, LA: Jacob Street (S1, E32), Hildi
Philadelphia, PA: Jeannes Street (S2, E10), Gen
Chicago, IL: Spaulding Avenue (S2, E15), Hildi
Seattle, WA: Dakota Street (S2, E22), Laurie
Texas: Sherwood Street (S2, E37), Gen
Plano, TX: Bent Horn Court (S2, E40), Gen
Plano, TX: Bent Horn Court (S2, E40), Vern
Plano, TX: Shady Valley Road (S2, E41), Hildi
Raleigh, NC: Legging Lane (S2, E43), Frank
Philadelphia, PA: 22nd Street (S3, E8), Gen
New Jersey: Manitoba Trail (S3, E13), Doug
Nazareth, PA: First Street (S3, E14), Doug
London, England: Garden Flat (S3, E26), Hildi
San Antonio, TX: Ghostbridge (S3, E29), Hildi
Miami, FL: Miami Place (S3, E44), Hildi
Florida: Night Owl Lane (S3, E47), Hildi
Los Angeles, CA: Irving Street (S3, E50), Gen
Orlando, FL: Winter Song Drive (S3, E53), Doug
Orlando, FL: Whisper Lake (S3, E54), Frank

Themed Rooms

New Orleans, LA: D'evereaux Street
    (S1, E34), Vern; Soccer
Boston, MA: Ashfield Street (S2, E7),
    Gen; Moroccan
Philadelphia, PA: Jeannes Street (S2, E10), Gen;
    Scrabble Board
Maryland: Fairway Court (S2, E13), Doug;
    Pullman Car
Colorado: Andes Way (S2, E19), Vern; Stripes

Outstanding Projects....

Orlando, FL: Winterhaven (SI, E29), Doug
Albuquerque, NM: Gloria (SI, E30), Doug
Providence, RI: Phillips Street (S2, E5), Vern
Philadelphia, PA: Jeannes Street (S2, EIO), Vern
Maryland: Village Green (S2, EI2), Gen
Maryland: Fairway Court (S2, EI3), Doug
Chicago, IL: Fairview Avenue (S2, EI6), Gen
Oregon: Alsea Court (S2, E25), Frank
Santa Clara, CA: Lafayette Street (S2, E27), Frank
Oakland, CA: Webster Street (S2, E3I), Hildi
Plano, TX: Shady Valley Road (S2, E4I), Doug
Portland, OR: Rosemont Avenue (S3, E2), Vern
Pennsylvania: Gorski Lane (S3, EIO), Frank
Pennsylvania: Gorski Lane (S3, EIO), Doug
New Jersey: Catania Court (S3, EI5), Hildi
California: Dusty Trail (S3, E34), Doug
California: Dusty Trail (S3, E34), Gen
Scottsdale, AZ: Bell Road (S3, E38), Vern
South Carolina: Sherborne Drive (S3, E56), Doug
Pennsylvania: Tremont Drive (S3, E57), Vern

Room Styles

Casual Rooms
Alpharetta, GA: Providence Oaks (SI, E4), Roderick
Lawrenceville, GA: Pine Lane (SI, E5), Hildi
Washington, D.C.: Cleveland Park (SI, E7), Doug
Philadelphia, PA: Valley Road (SI, EII), Doug
Philadelphia, PA: Galahad Road (SI, EI2), Gen
Knoxville, TN: Courtney Oak (SI, EI3), Frank
Knoxville, TN: Stubbs Bluff (SI, E20), Frank
Key West, FL: Elizabeth Street (SI, E23), Frank
Santa Fe, NM: Felize (SI, E3I), Gen
New Orleans, LA: D'evereaux Street (SI, E34), Gen
New Jersey: Tall Pines Drive (S2, E2), Laurie
Boston, MA: Institute Road (S2, E9), Frank
Philadelphia, PA: Jeannes Street (S2, EIO), Gen
Chicago, IL: Fairview Avenue (S2, EI6), Gen
Oregon: Alsea Court (S2, E25), Frank
Berkeley, CA: Prospect Street (S2, E30), Doug
Los Angeles, CA: Willoughby Avenue (S2, E33), Gen
Plano, TX: Bent Horn Court (S2, E40), Gen
Plano, TX: Shady Valley Road (S2, E4I), Doug
Raleigh, NC: Legging Lane (S2, E43), Frank
New York: Half Hollow Turn (S3, E7), Kia
New Jersey: Manitoba Trail (S3, EI3), Frank
California: Fairfield (S3, E35), Kia
Los Angeles, CA: Elm Street (S3, E48), Gen
Los Angeles, CA: Irving Street (S3, E50), Gen
Los Angeles, CA: Seventh Street (S3, E52), Edward
Orlando, FL: Winter Song Drive (S3, E53), Doug

Orlando, FL: Winter Song Drive (S3, E53), Vern
South Carolina: Sherborne Drive (S3, E56), Edward

Formal Rooms
Alpharetta, GA: Providence Oaks (SI, E4), Hildi
Buckhead, GA; Canter Road (SI, E6), Laurie
Philadelphia, PA: Valley Road (SI, EII), Laurie
Miami, FL: 168th/83rd Streets (SI, E2I), Laurie
Austin, TX: Wing Road (SI, E25), Hildi
Austin, TX: Birdhouse Drive (SI, E26), Laurie
Maple Glen, PA: Fiedler Road (S2, E3), Gen
Springfield, MA: Sunset Terrace (S2, E8), Hildi
Springfield, MA: Sunset Terrace (S2, E8), Vern
Philadelphia, PA: Jeannes Street (S2, EIO), Vern
Colorado: Berry Avenue (S2, EI7), Hildi
California: Peralta Street (S2, E32), Doug
Los Angeles, CA: Springdale Drive (S2, E34), Vern
Wake Forest, NC: Rodney Bay (S2, E45), Laurie
New Jersey: Manitoba Trail (S3, EI3), Doug
Mississippi: Golden Pond (S3, E27), Laurie
San Antonio, TX: Ghostbridge (S3, E29), Vern
Vegas, NV: Smokemont Court (S3, E4I), Laurie
South Carolina: Innisbrook Lane (S3, E55), Laurie
Pennsylvania: Tremont Drive (S3, E57), Vern
Pennsylvania: Bryant Court (S3, E58), Hildi

Chic & Modern Rooms
Philadelphia, PA: Strathmore Road (SI, EIO), Dez
Cincinnati, OH: Madison & Forest (SI, EI6), Doug
San Diego, CA: Elm Ridge (SI, EI7), Hildi
Albuquerque, NM: Gloria (SI, E30), Doug
New Orleans, LA: Jacob Street (SI, E32), Hildi
New Orleans, LA: D'evereaux Street (SI, E34), Vern
Quakertown, PA: Quakers Way (S2, EI), Hildi
Providence, RI: Phillips Street (S2, E5), Hildi
Maryland: Village Green (S2, EI2), Doug
Colorado: Cherry Street (S2, EI8), Laurie [Well,
    it's mod, anyway.]
California: Peralta Street (S2, E32), Hildi
Los Angeles, CA: Willoughby Avenue (S2, E33), Doug
California: Abbeywood Lane (S2, E35), Hildi
Philadelphia, PA: East Avenue (S3, EI6), Hildi
Scottsdale, AZ: Bell Road (S3, E38), Vern
Vegas, NV: Smokemont Courts (S3, E4I), Edward
Miami, FL: Ten Court (S3, E43), Hildi
Miramar, FL: Avenue 164 (S3, E45), Frank
Los Angeles, CA: Irving Street (S3, E50), Frank
South Carolina: Sherborne Drive (S3, E56), Doug
Pennsylvania: Tremont Drive (S3, E57), Gen
Pennsylvania: Bryant Court (S3, E58), Hildi
Pennsylvania: Cresheim Road (S3, E59), Hildi

Cottage/Country Rooms
Knoxville, TN: Fourth & Gill (SI, EI), Frank
Knoxville, TN: Forest Glen (SI, E2), Doug
Athens, GA: County Road (SI, E3), Frank
Lawrenceville, GA: Pine Lane (SI, E5), Hildi

Lawrenceville, GA: Pine Lane (SI, E5), Dez
Alexandria, VA: Riefton Court (SI, E8), Frank
Philadelphia, PA: Valley Road (SI, EII), Doug
Knoxville, TN: Courtney Oak (SI, EI3), Frank
Cincinnati, OH: Melrose Avenue (SI, EI4), Hildi
San Diego, CA: Elm Ridge (SI, EI7), Gen
Knoxville, TN: Stubbs Bluff (SI, E20), Doug
Key West, FL: Elizabeth Street (SI, E23), Gen
Key West, FL: Elizabeth Street (SI, E23), Frank
Orlando, FL: Winterhaven (SI, E29), Doug
New Jersey: Lincroft (SI, E39), Doug
New Jersey: Lincroft (SI, E39), Laurie
New Jersey: Lafayette Street (SI, E40), Frank
Northampton, PA: James Avenue (S2, E4), Frank
Providence, RI: Wallis Avenue (S2, E6), Frank
New Jersey: Perth Road (S2, EII), Frank
Chicago, IL: Edward Road (S2, EI4), Laurie
Seattle, WA: I37th Street (S2, E2I), Doug
Seattle, WA: I37th Street (S2, E2I), Frank
Santa Clara, CA: Lafayette Street (S2, E27), Frank
Maine: George Road (S3, EI), Gen
Long Island, NY: Steuben Boulevard (S3, E4), Frank
Philadelphia, PA: Gettysburg Lane (S3, E9), Frank
New Jersey: Manitoba Trail (S3, EI3), Frank

Exotic Rooms
California: Corte Rosa (S2, E28), Vern
California: Grenadine Way (S2, E29), Vern
Pennsylvania: Gorski Lane (S3, EIO), Doug
Indianapolis, IN: Halleck Way (S3, E22), Kia
Missouri: Sunburst Drive (S3, E23), Gen
San Clemente, CA: Camino Mojada (S3, E33), Gen
Scottsdale, AZ: Windrose Avenue (S3, E39), Frank
Miami, FL: Ten Court (S3, E43), Kia
Orlando, FL: Smith Street (S3, E46), Kia
Florida: Night Owl Lane (S3, E47), Edward

General Index

project index

Find the perfect decorating project fast and easy.